CREATIVE
CRAFTS
FOR KIDS

CREATIVE CRAFTS FOR KIDS

Over 100 fun projects for two to ten year olds

hamlyn

An Hachette UK Company
www.hachette.co.uk

First published in Great Britain in 2006 by
Hamlyn, a division of Octopus Publishing Group Ltd
Endeavour House, 189 Shaftesbury Avenue,
London WC2H 8JY
www.octopusbooks.co.uk

First published in paperback in 2009
Copyright © Octopus Publishing Group Ltd 2006,
2009

Gill Dickinson and Cheryl Owen assert the moral right
to be identified as the authors of this work.

ISBN: 978-0-600-61926-0

A CIP catalogue record for this book is available from
the British Library

Printed and bound in China

10 9 8 7 6 5 4

Some of the material in this book has appeared in
Crafts for Kids (Gill Dickinson), *Gifts for Kids to Make*
(Cheryl Owen), *Kids' Baking* (Sara Lewis) and *Kids in
the Kitchen* (Sara Lewis), also published by Hamlyn.

Disclaimer
The publishers cannot accept any legal responsibility
or liability for accidents or damage arising from the
use of any items mentioned in this book or in the
carrying out of any of the projects.

NOTES
Standard level spoon measures are used in all recipes:
1 tablespoon = one 15 ml spoon
1 teaspoon = one 5 ml spoon

Both metric and imperial measurements are given for the recipes.
Use one set of measures only, not a mixture of both.

Ovens should be preheated to the specified temperature.
If using a fan-assisted oven, follow the manufacturer's
instructions for adjusting the time and temperature.

Medium eggs have been used throughout.

A few recipes include nuts and nut derivatives. Anyone with a
known nut allergy must avoid these. Children under the age of
3 with a family history of nut allergy, asthma, eczema or any type
of allergy are also advised to avoid eating dishes which contain
nuts. Do not give whole nuts or seeds to any child under the age
of 5 because of risk of choking.

contents

introduction

Children love being creative, and this book contains masses of super gifts for youngsters aged from three to ten years old to make for family and friends. The simple projects in this book should be inspirational and fun to do, whether it's making a monster mask to wear at Halloween or sticking down brightly coloured paper to make a birthday card for a brother or sister.

Being able to create something special is important for everyone, but particularly so for children. They can start from a really young age, first by observing parents or siblings and gradually participating more and more until they have the satisfaction of producing something all by themselves. Once children have gained in confidence by making some of the projects, they can have fun adapting the ideas to create their own wonderful designs. To choose the colours and materials that they like should be a rewarding and satisfying part of the experience.

This book includes crafts to cater to all interests. There are projects to appeal to children who enjoy getting messy, involving clay and salt-dough modelling, and others ideas that suit those of a neat and tidy nature, including sewing and working with pressed flowers. There are also simple cooking projects and more unusual hobbies, such as making candles and fragrant toiletries.

Each chapter includes a variety of themed projects with easy-to-follow step-by-step instructions. Safety is a key issue, so adult supervision and assistance is always advisable, especially when cooking and using knives, scissors and dyes. It also helps to control the mess! The making times and age ranges are given as a loose guide, but be led by your child, and remember that most children will derive satisfaction from even the tiniest contribution. Guides to the age range and time needed are given with each project, but they are loose guides, so you should be led by your child's abilities.

craft materials

At the start of each project is a list of all the items you need, many of which you will already have around the house. Remember that all sorts of materials can be recycled for craftwork, such as glass jars, egg cartons, kitchen roll and snack tubes. Also, keep odd buttons and scraps of fabric, ribbons, lace, beads and sequins.

paper

Most craft projects will require you to use paper at some point. Fortunately, it is versatile and strong. Coloured tissue, crêpe, patterned, tracing and parcel papers are usually available at most art and craft shops. Papers can be cut, punched, folded, torn, scrunched-up or even used as a stencil. Always have a selection handy and keep any scraps that are left over.

paints and pens

Acrylic paint is recommended for most of the painted projects. Although it is not the cheapest paint, a little goes a long way, the colours mix easily and dry quickly, and it is non-toxic. For special effects such as papier-mâché jewellery, there are fluorescent acrylics. Poster paint is inexpensive, readily available and suits many paper, card and clay projects. Many ceramic paints can be fixed by heating in an oven (this makes the object dishwasher-proof) - follow the manufacturer's instructions. Source paint for decorating ceramics and fabric at art shops.

Decorating with fabric dyes, paints and felt-tipped pens is fun but it can also be messy. Glow-in-the-dark and 3-D puff paints are perfect for the Halloween costumes, not to mention other projects.

Felt-tipped pens, coloured wax and chalk crayons are always a good standby and can be used in conjunction with other materials.

glues

PVA glue is non-toxic, very strong and can be used for most of the projects in this book. Always use stick glue on tissue and crêpe paper as water-based glues (such as PVA) and paints dissolve them.

Glitter glues are usually non-toxic and they come in amazing colours from primary and metallic to iridescent greens and blues. These glues are simple and safe to use and look stunning when dry. If a project is looking a little dull, jazz it up with a touch of glitter glue and you will be surprised at the result.

- When buying tools or materials, always check that they are safe for children and non-toxic.

- Keep the room well ventilated when working with adhesive, acrylic paint and cosmetic colours. Wash hands well with soap and water after use.

- Supervise young or less careful children carefully if they are working on a project that calls for knives, sharp scissors, a needle or cooking over heat.

- Never leave scissors open or lying where younger children or pets can reach them.

- Always stick needles and pins into a pin cushion or a scrap of cloth when not in use.

- Cover work surfaces with newspaper or an old cloth, preferably plastic. Plastic bags cut open and laid flat make a good water-resistant surface. Keep kitchen towels or rags at hand to mop up spills. Protect clothing with an apron or wear old clothes.

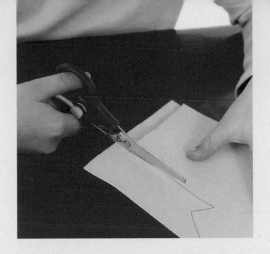

- Wash paintbrushes immediately after use: modern paints dry quickly and dried-on paint can ruin a brush. Always replace tops on pens, paint and glue containers.

modelling materials

Air-drying clay can be rolled, modelled or shaped over a mould such as a bowl. Leave to harden, then paint. Polymer clay comes in many colours; why not mix them for a marbled effect? This clay is hardened by baking. Salt dough is made from plain flour, salt and water. Younger children enjoy stamping out shapes with cookie cutters. Once modelled, bake very slowly in the oven. Paint when cool. Applying a few coats of varnish prolongs the life of a baked salt-dough item, but don't display in a steamy or damp place!

specialist items

Pipe cleaners, chenilles and strawers are essential for the craft box: they can be bent, curled, cut, and used by young and old alike. They are useful for a wide range of ideas, tied round a gift instead of a ribbon, threaded with beads for a necklace or used for a three-dimensional card.

Coloured glitters, beads and sequins can be added as a finishing touch to many projects. None of these tiny glittery items should ever be left in the hands of very young children but used only in the presence of an adult.

Pre-cut foam shapes, self-stick notes and bags of mixed gummed paper shapes are brilliant for children to use. They get instant results and feel they are participating with older members of the family by decorating a birthday card, making paper bunting or a piece of jewellery. Although not as creative as using other materials, ready-made items are bright and appealing and can be made into something quickly, which can be beneficial especially when very small children are involved.

kids in the kitchen

Cooking is great fun for kids. There are lots of delicious recipes in this book, so there you're bound to find something that your child would like to make. Once they've chosen a recipe, make sure that there is time to prepare and cook it and collect together all the necessary ingredients and equipment.

basic equipment

Most of the equipment used in this book will be the kind of things that you have at home already. The required equipment (and ingredients) are listed in order of use in the recipes in this book. Microwaves and electric mixers have been given as options to help save time and effort but are not essential.

weighing and measuring

Careful measuring of ingredients is vital for successful results - this sounds boring, but it's true. The recipes are written in both metric and imperial measurements. Whichever one you choose to follow, stick with the same one all through the recipe, don't mix and match.

Weighing and measuring can also be educational, helping to teach children:

- co-ordination
- the importance of accuracy
- basic number and addition skills
- the idea of volume

…without their really realizing it!

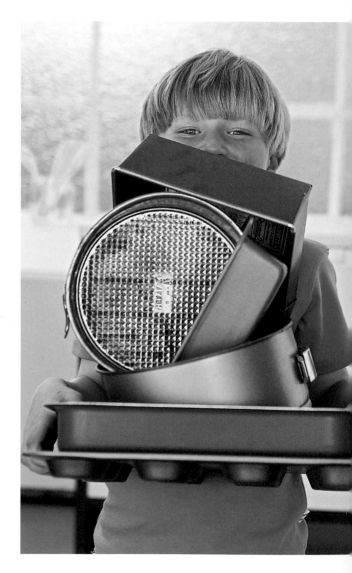

cooking with very little children

Young children need supervision in the kitchen at all times. Stand your child on a sturdy chair so that he or she can reach the work surface or sink. Alternatively, cover the floor with a plastic or PVC tablecloth then get the child to measure and mix while sitting on the cloth.

Some little children really hate the feel of PVC aprons. If you don't have a cotton one that's small enough then use an old shirt of an older brother or sister as a cover up. Remember to allow plenty of time for your cooking as kids hate to be hurried.

When the cooking's done, it's good practice to involve little ones in the clearing up, too. Even tiny children can have a go at washing up if you give them plenty of encouragement and keep the mop handy for sorting out any spills.

clearing up!

The tidying up afterwards is never as much fun as the cooking but it has to be done! Encourage your child to help you put away all unused ingredients, wash up and dry all the equipment used and wipe all the work surfaces with a clean damp cloth before leaving the kitchen.

HYGIENE AND SAFETY TIPS

Don't forget the following basic hygiene and safety rules when working in the kitchen:

- Always wash your hands before you begin.

- Tie back long hair.

- Wear an apron or old shirt to keep clothes clean.

- Only use food that is within its 'use-by' date and throw away any food that has been dropped on the floor.

- Supervise children carefully if a project calls for sharp knives, electrical equipment or the cooker.

- If you're not sure what size saucepan to use, then choose a bigger one so that its contents will be less likely to boil over. Turn saucepan handles to the side of the cooker, to avoid them being knocked as you pass by.

- Wipe up any spilt food or liquids on the floor at once to avoid slipping on a greasy patch.

- Always use oven gloves when taking hot dishes out of the oven.

- Avoid damaging the work surface with sharp knives or hot dishes – always chop or cut food on a chopping board and put hot baking tins or saucepans on a heatproof mat, a wooden chopping board, or even the hob as long as nothing is cooking on it.

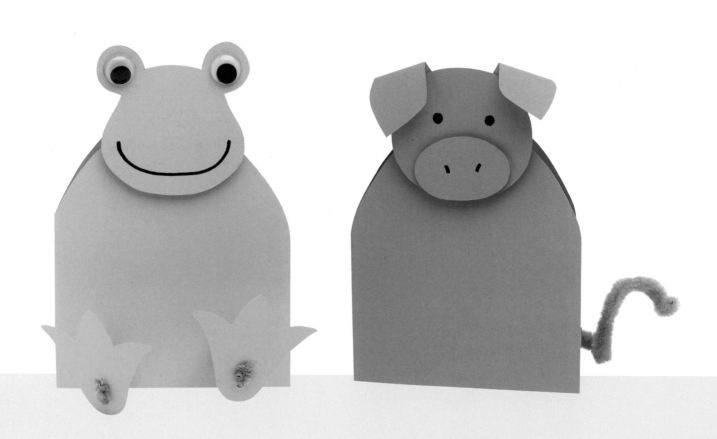

fun with paper

T-shirt card

ages 5–6 years

This card and the variations all resemble clothing and are folded in half so they stand up. They offer a great opportunity to gather scraps of fabric, buttons, braid and lace to make an original card that will be worth having as a keepsake.

(**1**) Make sure the white paper is large enough for your card. Cut a piece of fabric to exactly the same size as the paper. Glue the fabric smoothly, right side up, onto the card.

(**2**) Draw a T-shirt shape onto the fabric from the template on page 240.

(**3**) Cut carefully around the outline. Then fold the card in half, and cut out the neckline.

**time needed
30 minutes**

what you need

Thick white paper

Fabric scrap (large enough for card)

Scissors

Glue

Pencil

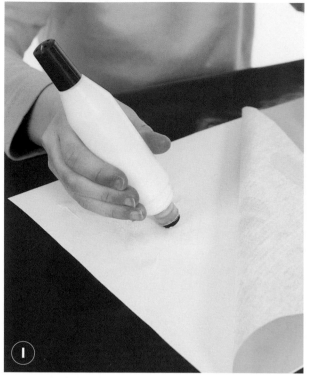

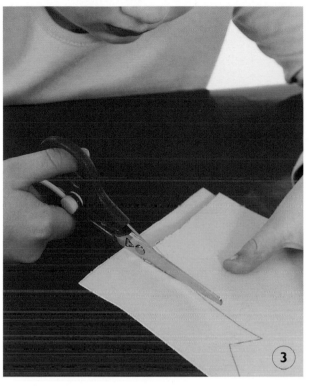

(3)

variations

You can be really creative with these clothing cards. Either use the template provided, or make up your own shapes, such as a shoe with laces, or a baseball cap. Here are some ideas to try:

• Felt hat with sequins and feathers.

• Cotton apron with lace trims and pockets.

• Boxer shorts with buttons and ribbon.

• Handbag with pompom and coloured pipe cleaners.

tips
★ Apply the glue to the paper rather than the fabric. Make sure you spread it evenly.
★ Don't be over-ambitious size-wise. It's easier to stick the fabric to a small area.

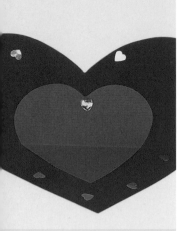

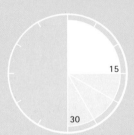

valentine cards

ages 2–6 years

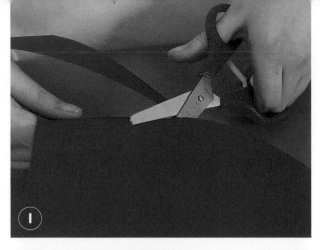
1

Everyone loves to receive a special handmade card especially on Valentine's Day. There is something here for all the family to make. Furry pipe cleaners with folded arms and hands are great for the younger members, while the older children tackle the more sophisticated glitter hearts and lips. All the cards take only a few minutes to make.

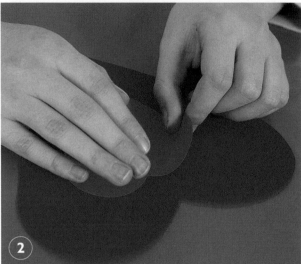
2

1 Cut a red heart out of paper using the larger template on page 241.

2 Place a pink self-stick note in the centre of the card. If you cannot find these, draw and cut out a smaller heart from pink paper using the smaller template on page 241.

3 Fold the card in half so that it sits up on a flat surface.

4

4 Decorate with diamantés and sequins using dabs of glue.

time needed
15–30 minutes

what you need

Scissors

Red paper

Pink heart-shaped
self-stick notes
(or pink paper)

Sequins and diamantés

Glue

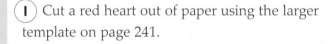

variations

hugs and kisses

Younger children will love making coloured hearts from pipe cleaners, with folded arms and hands glued on.

happy heart

Decorate a card heart with a face. Stick it onto a contrasting card at a jaunty angle. Add long folded legs with feet, for that special person in your life.

zigzag card

Stick decorated hearts to the top of twisted pipe cleaners and add them to the folds of a zigzag silver card for a multi-dimensional treat.

tip
★ Self-stick notes are a good quick alternative to making your own cut-out shapes.

what you need

Red paper

Pencil

Scissors

Black felt-tipped pen

Black tissue or crêpe paper

Stick glue

Hole punch

Red ribbon

ladybird gift tag

ages 2–6 years

Handmade paper tags will make any gift extra special and they can be made by children of all ages. Recycled food cans filled with bright spring flowers or bulbs make wonderful Mother's Day gifts; you can tie the gift tag onto a leaf or flowerhead.

(1) Fold a piece of red paper in half. Draw half a ladybird shape onto the paper – a plump semicircle with a slightly pointed end. Cut out the ladybird shape.

2 Use the black felt-tipped pen to draw a line down the middle of the red shape for wings and colour in the head.

(3) Roll about eight small balls of black tissue or crêpe paper and glue them onto the ladybird.

(4) Punch a hole through the head of the ladybird and thread a ribbon through it for the tag.

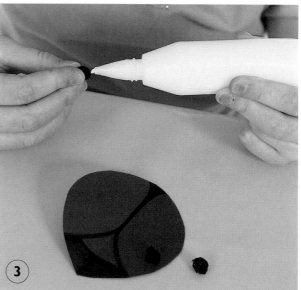

variations

You can make tags in a variety of shapes and sizes: butterflies, bees, fish and flowers, for example. Use contrasting torn paper and tissue paper for decoration.

tips

★ Simple distinctive shapes work best and give quick results, especially satisfying for younger children.
★ Always fold card or paper in half then cut out shapes to ensure a symmetrical outline.
★ Paper is very strong. Try rolling it to make different shapes to glue onto your tag.

10

30

**time needed
10–30 minutes**

what you need

Poster paint

Rolls or sheets of
coloured paper

Brushes

Scissors

Glue

Card

Ribbon, chenille or
pipe cleaners

gift wrap
and tags

ages 2–6 years

Making colourful wrapping paper is a
wonderful project for a fine summer's
day. Lay your paper outside with pots of
coloured paints and enjoy marking the
paper with different brush strokes. You
can also make gift tags out of the same
decorated paper threaded with ribbon
or chenille. If you do this project
indoors make sure that you cover all
nearby surfaces!

(**1**) Dab paint circles onto plain coloured paper
at even intervals. Leave to dry.

(**2**) Make a gift tag by by cutting the painted
paper to size. Glue the tag onto card if the
paper is thin. Punch a hole for the tie to
go through.

(**3**) Make interesting ties from ribbon, chenille
or pipe cleaners.

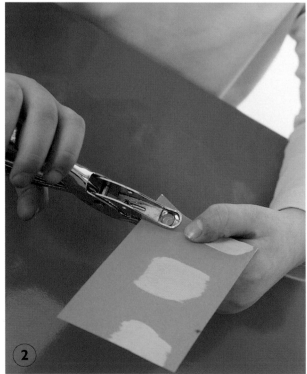

variations

- Contrasting colours work well for gift wrap. Try green and orange, bright blue or a paler blue background.

- Experiment with painting dots, squares, stripes and crosses.

- Make matching cards, paper, tags and envelopes using self-adhesive dots and stars.

- Choose ribbons that make the colours look even brighter, such as day-glow green or pink.

candy bags

ages 4–6 years

These decorative baskets can be filled with any sort of candy or a small gift and wrapped or tied in a little piece of coloured net.

(1) Take a square of yellow paper and cut along one edge with zigzag scissors. Form the basket shape by wrapping the zigzag edge of the paper around the bottom half of a beaker placed upside-down on the table. Tape the seam together and fold the free section of the paper over the bottom of the beaker to make the base of the basket. Secure with tape.

(2) Cut a small strip of paper to be used for the handle using zigzag scissors and staple into position on each side of the basket.

(3) Using ordinary scissors, cut a small fan-shaped piece of paper for a tail (don't forget to cut in the feathers) and two small wings. Glue the tail to the back of the basket, and the wings to either side, just beneath the handle.

(4) Make eyes, a beak and a tuft of head feathers out of felt or paper and glue them onto the pompom head. When they are dry, glue the head onto the front of the basket.

(5) Buy chocolate-covered eggs or other small gifts. Wrap them in a small piece of net, tie with a bow and place inside your basket.

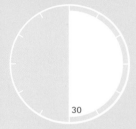

30

time needed
30 minutes

what you need

Yellow paper

Scissors: zigzag and ordinary

Beaker

Sticky tape

Stapler

Glue

Yellow pompom for head

Felt or paper for eyes and beak

Chocolate eggs or small gift

Net

Ribbon

22

variations

• Making different shapes and animals makes this project fun for all the family. The baskets can be any shape or size but try and stick to an Easter theme, keeping the colours soft and pretty.

• Look out for boxes, bowls and anything that will make an interesting shape to use as a mould for your baskets.

tip
★ Make sure that the paper is secured properly at the base of the basket and that the handles are secure.

what you need

Orange card

Scissors

2 small potatoes

Knife or apple corer

Poster paint (four
  different colours)

Brush

Black felt-tipped pen

polka dot rabbit card

ages 2–6 years

Make a simple, brightly decorated, stamped card to give to friends and family at Eastertime. You can make stamps by cutting up vegetables such as potatoes and carrots or cutting a shape out of a sponge, or simply buying ready-made stamps from an art shop. This is fun and easy to do, as long as you don't mind the mess!

1 Using the template on page 242, cut a rabbit out of orange card.

2 Cut the potatoes in half and on each half score a small circle with a knife (or an apple corer). Then cut away around it to leave a raised circle.

3 Use four contrasting colours of poster paint, one for each potato circle. Dab paint onto the potato circles with a brush and stamp over the orange card.

4 When the paint is dry, fold the card in half, then fold each edge back towards the middle fold so the card can stand up. Draw on a face with a black felt-tipped pen.

variations

coloured cards and tags

Stick a contrasting strip of paper onto a folded card. Cut out
your stamped image and glue it into the centre of the card.
Decorate with beads and sequins. Make a tag by threading
a ribbon through a punched hole.

tips

★ Make a circle stamp by cutting a carrot in half
  and using the cut end.
★ Keep different coloured paint in separate
  containers and use a separate brush for each
  one so the colours stay bright and clean.
★ When stamping onto dark back-grounds, mix
  white paint into coloured paints.

rocking cards

ages 2–6 years

Handmade cards and gift tags are inexpensive to make and a must at Christmas. Younger children will love these rocking Christmas cards, while coloured bands to wrap around boxes, and tags attached to brightly coloured ribbons will make any gift look special. Decorative punches with many designs can be bought from art shops and give hours of pleasure as they are so easy to use.

time needed
30 minutes

what you need
Scissors
Coloured paper
Star punch
Silver star

(1) Cut a circle out of coloured paper (draw around a small plate to make a template) and fold it in half. Punch stars around the edge of the semicircle.

(2) Cut out a star (see page 238 for template) in another colour. Stick it to the middle of the folded edge with glue.

(3) Add a silver star to the centre of the star.

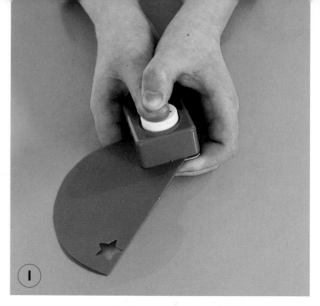

①

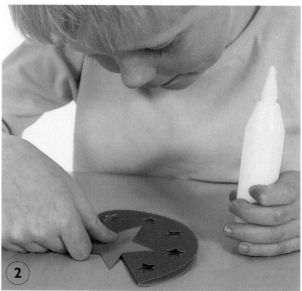

②

③

variations

design your own card

Customize rocking cards for any occasion by sticking different shapes on to the fold. You can use the templates on pages 238–239 for Christmas shapes.

gift tags

Tags are so quick to make if you use lots of different shapes and coloured papers. Simply punch and stick for an amazing variety.

tips
★ Pre-cut shapes such as self-stick notes make cards and tags even quicker to assemble.
★ Use bright, contrasting coloured papers for the best effect.

wrap it up

Make inexpensive gift wrap by covering a box in coloured paper and adding a contrasting band with glued on trees or other decorations.

revolving letter card

ages 2–6 years

Personalize a birthday card or invitation by placing a number or letter on a contrasting background; attach it with a press stud or paper fastener through the centre so it revolves. Everyone loves to receive a handmade card, parents and grandparents alike. Keep colours clean and fresh and perhaps buy a bright coloured envelope to pop your card in.

(1) Draw a large capital letter on a piece of purple paper and cut it out with scissors or a craft knife.

(2) Stick on pre-cut gummed shapes or flowers to decorate.

(3) Place the letter in the centre of a card in a contrasting colour, here green. Punch a hole through both the card and the letter and place the press stud into position.

**time needed
30 minutes**

what you need

Paper

Pencil

Craft knife or scissors

Pre-gummed shapes

Card

Hole punch

Stud or paper fastener

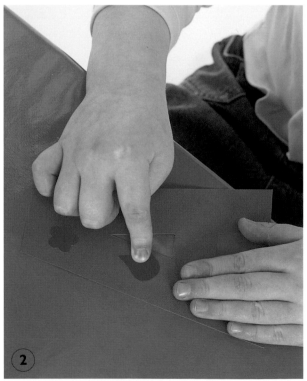

variations

- These cards can be made in all shapes and sizes. Make a round one and cut around the circle with zigzag scissors, or punch holes around the edge with a hole punch.

- A teddy bear, robot, boat or any shape you fancy could be used instead of a letter or number.

- Glue strips of patterned paper onto a plain card before adding your revolving shape.

tip
★ Use pre-cut gummed shapes for quickness, but you can always design and stick on your own.

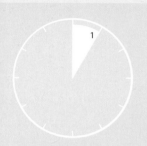

**time needed
1 hour**

what you need

Ruler

Pencil

Scissors

Light brown card

Tracing paper

Black felt-tipped pen

Black paper

PVA glue

Black pompom

2 joggle eyes

2 hook and loop spot
fasteners

spotty dog card

ages 6–8 years

The head of this amusing character is attached with hook and loop spot fasteners so it can be removed and worn as a badge – the spot fasteners fix onto any woolly surface. (Buy them from craft shops.) As a variation you can make a pink pig or a funny frog.

I Cut an 18 x 11 cm (7¼ x 4½ in) rectangle from the light brown card and fold it in half, parallel with the short edges. Trace the body template on page 248 then transfer the design to the folded card, matching the fold lines. Cut out the body. Cut a head and tail from light brown card too, using the templates provided.

2 Draw a mouth on the head with the black felt-tipped pen. Tear black paper into patches. Glue the patches to the head, body and tail.

3 Glue the black pompom to the middle of the head as a nose. Glue the joggle eyes above the nose.

4 Using the template on page 248, cut out two ears from the black paper. Glue the ears behind the head. Fold the tips of the ears over the head.

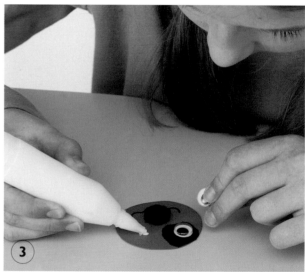

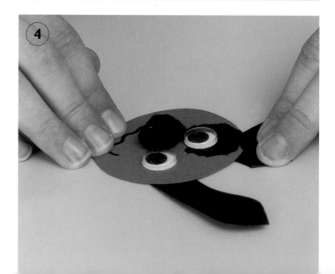

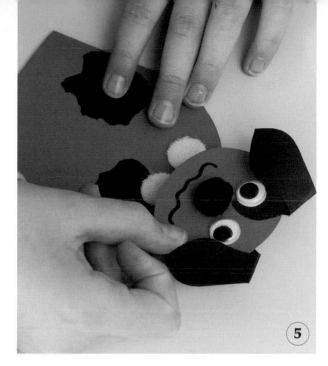

variations

pink pig card

Using the templates on pages 248–249, cut a body and pig head, muzzle and ears from pink card. Draw eyes on the head and nostrils on the muzzle with a black felt-tipped pen. Stick the ears to the back of the head, and bend forward. Stick the muzzle to the head using a foam adhesive pad. Make a hole on the back of the body and fix a pink curly pipecleaner inside it as a tail.

funny frog card

Use the templates on pages 248–249 to cut out the frog's body, head and two feet from green card. Draw a smile on the head with a black felt-tipped pen. Glue two joggle eyes to the head. Make two holes on the front of the body and through the feet and fix a green pipecleaner between them for legs.

(**5**) Glue the tail to the back of the body and fold it toward the front. Stick the soft spot fasteners to the top of the body. Stick the head on top with the rough spot fasteners.

tip
★ If you prefer, you can draw the dog's patches with a black felt-tipped pen instead of gluing on torn paper.

what you need

Scissors

Pencil

Ruler

Crepe paper

All-purpose household
  glue

20 cm (8 in) narrow
  red braid

Shaped sequins

paper
handbag

ages 5–6 years

Slip a secret message or a tiny light-weight present into a pretty handbag decorated with colourful sequins. Use these paper creations as party bags for small, thin gifts, such as stickers and hair accessories. Friends are sure to love them! As a plus, the bag can be hung up and so makes a super Christmas tree decoration.

1 Cut a 20 x 10 cm (8 x 4 in) rectangle of crepe paper, cutting the long edge parallel with the ridges on the paper. Fold the paper in half.

2 Using a pencil and ruler, draw slanted edges from the fold out to the top corners. Cut along the slanted edges.

3 Gently stretch both sides of the top to make a pretty frilled edge.

4 Glue the slanted edges together. Glue one end of the braid inside each corner of the top of the bag to make a handle.

5 Decorate by sticking rows of sequins across the front of the bag.

2

3

4

variations

lilac handbag

Fold the paper rectangle in step 1 but do not
cut slanted side edges or stretch the top of the
bag. Glue the sides together, then give the bag
a beaded braid handle. Glue lilac marabou trim
around the top edge and decorate by sticking a
few silver sequins on the front.

turquoise handbag

In step 2 draw slanted side edges down and
outward from the top edge to the fold. Gently
stretch both sides of the top to make a frilled
edge. Glue the sides together, then give the bag
a gold braid handle. Apply wavy lines of glitter
across the bag.

tips
★ Crepe paper folds more neatly if
  you draw along the fold line
  first with a pencil.
★ Try using double-layered crepe
  paper: it's stronger than a single
  layer and allows you to have a
  different colour showing on
  each side.

decorated notebook

ages 6–8 years

Ordinary notebooks are cheap to buy, but you can make them look very expensive by decorating them with strips of coloured paper. Save wrapping paper from birthdays and old scraps of wallpaper and tear out pages from glossy magazines with striking images. Cut the edges of some of the papers with deckle and zig-zag scissors for extra interest.

(1) Using the pen and ruler, draw lines on the plain and patterned papers, marking them into strips. Cut out the strips with the deckle-edged, zig-zag or ordinary scissors.

(2) Glue the strips to the front of the notebook and along the spine, leaving the ends extending above and below the cover.

(3) Open the book and glue the ends of the strips to the inside of the cover and spine.

(4) Measure the inside of the covers and, using ordinary scissors, cut two pieces of patterned paper to fit inside the covers. Glue the papers inside the covers to hide the ends of the strips. Leave open to dry.

45

**time needed
45 minutes**

what you need

Pen

Ruler

Plain and patterned papers

Scissors: deckle-edged, zig-zag and ordinary

Paper glue

Thick notebook with a spine

①

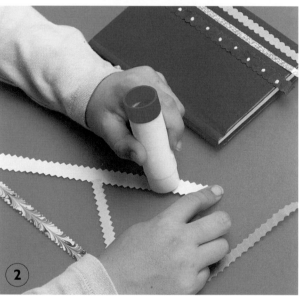

②

③

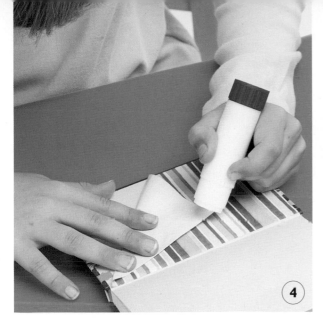

variations

striped writing paper and paper squares notelet

Glue strips of patterned papers and gift-wrapping ribbon along one edge of a piece of writing paper. Glue squares of patterned papers to the front of a notelet. Leave to dry before using.

ribbon, sequin and ric-rac notelet

Glue lengths of patterned ribbon and ric-rac and a string of sequins in stripes to the front of a notelet. Set aside until completely dry.

spotty writing paper and envelope

Attach round stickers to the top of a piece of writing paper. Reserve another sticker to fasten the envelope.

tip
★ Fold sheets of writing paper in half to make notelets, then decorate them.

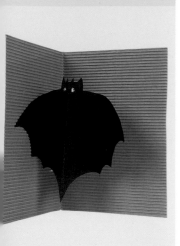

halloween invitations

ages 4–6 years

Halloween parties are always exciting, especially as there are so many spooky delights to make for them. Stick to a colour scheme of black and orange and keep all the family busy and amused preparing party bags, cards and invitations for the special day.

1 Fold a piece of black paper in half. Using the template on page 245, draw half a bat shape on the folded paper with a white pencil. Cut it out.

2 Make the eyes with silver glitter glue. Fold each wing back towards the centre fold.

3 Unfold the bat and glue the tip of each wing to each side of a folded orange piece of corrugated card. Make sure the centre fold of the bat is on the centre fold of the card.

**time needed
15 minutes**

what you need

Black paper

White pencil

Scissors

Silver glitter glue

Orange corrugated card

Glue

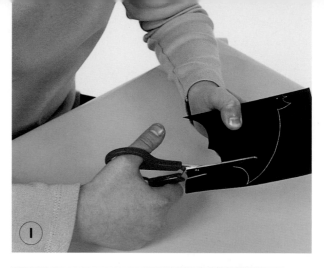

1

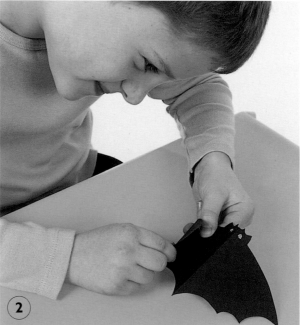

2

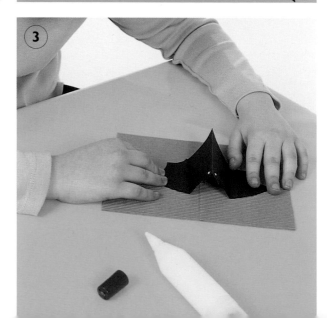

3

variations

party bags

Decorate small cones with black cut-outs of a cat's head (using the template on page 245). Make a sack from a length of crêpe paper folded and glued (using stick glue) along three sides; decorate it and fasten with wool, adding a slimy clip-on frog.

more scary cards

A simple black pumpkin (using the template on page 141) face will look stunning glued onto an orange card. Cut out a gruesome hand and give it glitter veins and spider ring (using the templates on pages 244 and 245).

tip
* Use a glue stick on crêpe paper – water-based glues dissolve and discolour the paper.

floral gift tag

ages 6–8 years

Receiving a present is always a treat, and to have a handmade gift tag attached is a super finishing touch. This gift tag with its pretty flower in a plant pot is so easy to make because the flower is just a square of scrunched-up tissue paper.

1 Cut a 12 x 8.5 cm (4¾ x 3⅜ in) rectangle of white card for the gift tag and fold it in half. Trace the plant pot template on page 247 then transfer the design on to the red corrugated card. Cut out the pot.

2 Glue the plant pot to the front of the tag.

3 Draw a plant stem and leaves from the top of the plant pot with the green felt-tipped pen.

4 Cut a 4 cm (1½ in) square of pink tissue paper. Scrunch up the square and glue to the top of the stem.

5 Punch a hole in the top left corner of the gift tag. Thread the red ribbon through the hole ready to tie to the present.

**time needed
45 minutes**

what you need

Ruler

Pencil

Scissors

White card

Tracing paper

Red corrugated card

Paper glue

Green felt-tipped pen

Pink tissue paper

Hole punch

20 cm (8 in) narrowred ribbon

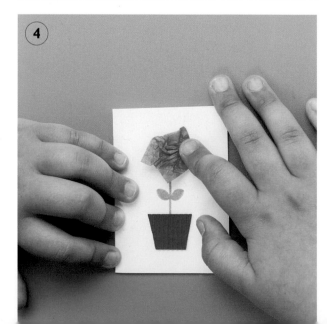

(5)

tip
★ If you can't source coloured corrugated card, cut out a piece of plain card from an old box and paint it brightly.

variations

tree in a tub picture

Cut a tub shape from pink corrugated card and glue it to a piece of cream card. Draw in the tree trunk with a green felt-tipped pen. Cut four 4 cm (1½ in) squares of green tissue paper and scrunch them to make the leaves. For the flowers cut out three 3 cm (1¼ in) squares of red tissue paper and scrunch them up. Glue the leaves then the flowers to the tree trunk. Glue the cream card to green chequered gift wrap and place inside a green picture frame.

yellow flower picture

Draw a row of three plant stems and leaves with a green felt-tipped pen on a piece of white card. Cut three 4 cm (1½ in) squares of yellow tissue paper, scrunch them up and glue to the stems. Stick the white card to red chequered gift wrap and place inside a picture frame.

button bear card

ages 3–5 years

Buttons come in so many colours, shapes and sizes and you are sure to have some spare ones at home. Have fun arranging the most colourful and unusual in different shapes to make amusing characters like this cute bear on a greetings card.

I Cut a 20 x 10 cm (8 x 4 in) rectangle of cream card to make the greetings card and fold it in half. Glue a pink button with four holes to the front of the card to make the bear's head.

2 Glue a larger red button beneath the head to make the body.

3 Stick two mauve buttons on each side of the body to form legs.

4 Glue two smaller purple buttons on each side at the top of the head to make ears. Finally, glue a very small pale pink button to the bottom of the head to create the bear's muzzle. Allow the glue to dry before writing inside the card.

45

**time needed
45 minutes**

what you need

Ruler

Pencil

Scissors

Cream card

Selection of flat buttons

All-purpose household glue

variations

dolphin card

Glue a dolphin-shaped button to the front of a pale blue card folded in half as before. Stick torn strips of bright blue and yellow paper across the card to create the sea and sand. To complete the picture, sew two shell-shaped buttons to the sand, being careful not to crease the card (an adult might need to help).

piggy card

Tear strips of lilac and spotty green paper, then glue them across the front of a pale blue folded card to make the sky and a field. Carefully sew three piggy-shaped buttons to the field.

tip
★ Buttons with flat backs can be glued in place but buttons with a shank, or raised part, on the back should be sewn to the card.

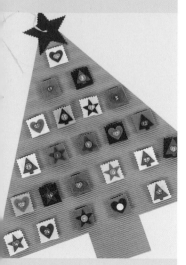

time needed
2–3 hours

what you need

Green corrugated card, 50 cm (20 in) square

Pencil

Scissors (ordinary and zigzag)

Coloured felts

Hole punch

Glue

Three-dimensional puff paint, availablefrom art shops (or marker pen)

Foam shapes

Velcro dots

24 trinkets or sweets

Cord

advent calendar

ages 5–6 years

Why not make your own Advent calender and fill each felt pocket with a tiny trinket or sweet?

(1) Cut a tree shape out of the green card. With zigzag scissors, cut out a pink felt star (see page 238 for template) and glue to the top of the tree. Punch a hole through the centre of the star.

(2) Use the small tree, heart and star templates on pages 238–239 to cut out 24 shapes from different-coloured felts (with ordinary scissors).

(3) Draw 24 oblong shapes – 2.5 cm x 7 cm (1 in x 3 in) – on different coloured felts. Cut them out with zigzag scissors. Apply glue to the long edges of the felt oblongs, fold over and press together to make a small felt bag.

(4) With puff paint or a marker pen, write the numbers 1 to 24 on small foam shapes. Glue each one onto a felt shape and then glue the felt shapes onto the little bags.

(5) Place the Velcro base dots onto the tree at even intervals. Place the other halves of the Velcro dots onto the underside of the 24 felt bags. Insert the trinkets or sweets into the felt bags and press into place on the calendar. Thread a cord through the hole at the top.

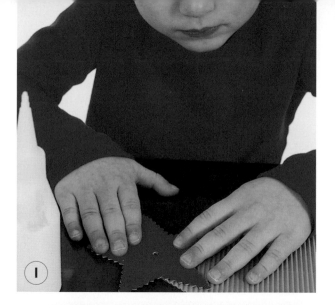

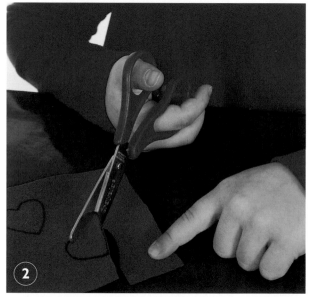

tips
★ Use ready-printed numbers for speed.
★ Substitute chocolates for the felt pockets on the tree, if you are short of time.

variation

chocolate calendar

Tape ribbon loops to the back of 24 Christmassy chocolate shapes. Write the numbers 1 to 24 on small adhesive dots and stick one onto each chocolate. Peg the chocolates up in order on a length of decorative ribbon.

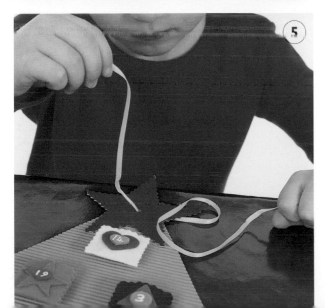

dazzling decorations

easter egg bunny

ages 2–6 years

These decorated eggs make an ideal gift for children to give to friends and relations on Easter Sunday.

1 To blow your own eggs, take a pin and pierce either end of the egg (this is a delicate operation and should be performed by an adult or with adult supervision). Blow through the top hole with a straw until the contents have run out, then rinse thoroughly with cold water and leave to dry.

2 Paint the eggs and leave to dry. You may need a couple of coats to cover completely.

3 While the paint is drying, cut out felt shapes for the ears, whiskers, nose, eyes and mouth.

④ When the paint is dry, glue the ears into position, folding back the lower end so that they rest on top of the egg. Glue on whiskers, eyes, a nose and mouth. Leave to dry.

5 Dab a little glue on the end of the plastic straw and insert the tip through the bottom of the egg and leave to dry.

⑥ As a finishing touch, tie a ribbon around the top of the straw and add a felt flower between the ears or at the front of the neck.

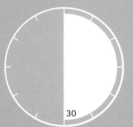

**time needed
30 minutes**

what you need

12 large eggs, if using real ones (to allow for breakages) or 6 plastic or polystyrene eggs

Large pin

Paints and paint brushes

Scissors

Felt

PVA glue

Glass beads or buttons

Plastic drinking straw

Narrow ribbon

(4)

(4)

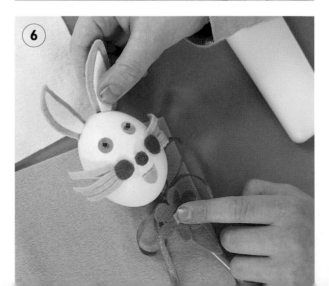

(6)

variations

jewelled eggs

These are simple but effective – choose sequins, glass beads or whatever takes your fancy and simply stick them onto the painted eggs. Thread a piece of ribbon through the holes and tie a knot at the bottom so that you can hang up the eggs.

jelly eggs

If you wish, you can fill the blown eggs with liquid jelly, then leave them in the refrigerator overnight to set.

funny faces

Instead of painting the eggs, leave the shells plain to mimic skin tone. Use wool or straw for the hair and stick on buttons, felt or pipe cleaners for the features.

tips
★ You can buy egg-blowing kits from craft catalogues or buy ready-blown eggs from garden centres.
★ To make paint stick to the eggshells, mix it with a little washing-up liquid.

paper chick frieze

ages 4–6 years

Seasonal paper cut-outs make an ideal table or window decoration. They can be as simple or as complicated as you like: decorate just with felt-tipped pens, or more elaborately with cut paper, self-adhesive shapes, wool and ribbon. Wrap a frieze around a box and secure with sticky tape to decorate a gift, or cut off one of the shapes and glue it onto a folded card.

(**1**) Take a long strip of yellow paper, about 70 cm x 10 cm (28 in x 4 in), and fold it evenly concertina style. You need six folds to give seven chicks, seven folds to give eight chicks, and so on. Make sure the folds align exactly.

(**2**) Draw around the template on page 243, positioning the point of the beak against one fold and the base of the tail against the other. Cut out the chick, taking care not to cut through the folds at the beak tip and on the tail.

(**3**) Unfold the frieze. Draw an eye and a wing on each chick with black felt-tipped pen and glue a feather on each tail.

**time needed
30 minutes**

what you need
Yellow paper

Scissors

Glue

Feathers

Black felt-tipped pen

Pencil

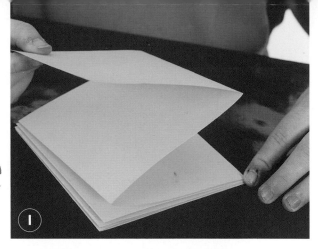

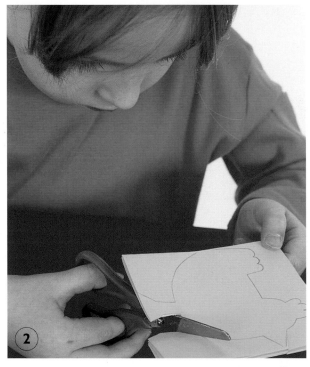

variations

egg extravaganza

Jazz up a simple egg frieze by decorating it with
coloured dots, beads, sequins and cut-out
squares and other shapes.

holding hands

This shape (see the template on page 242) is a
little more difficult to cut out. Younger children
can help to decorate it by gluing on
yellow hair, making aprons from
net or a doily and gluing on a
waistband and shoes.

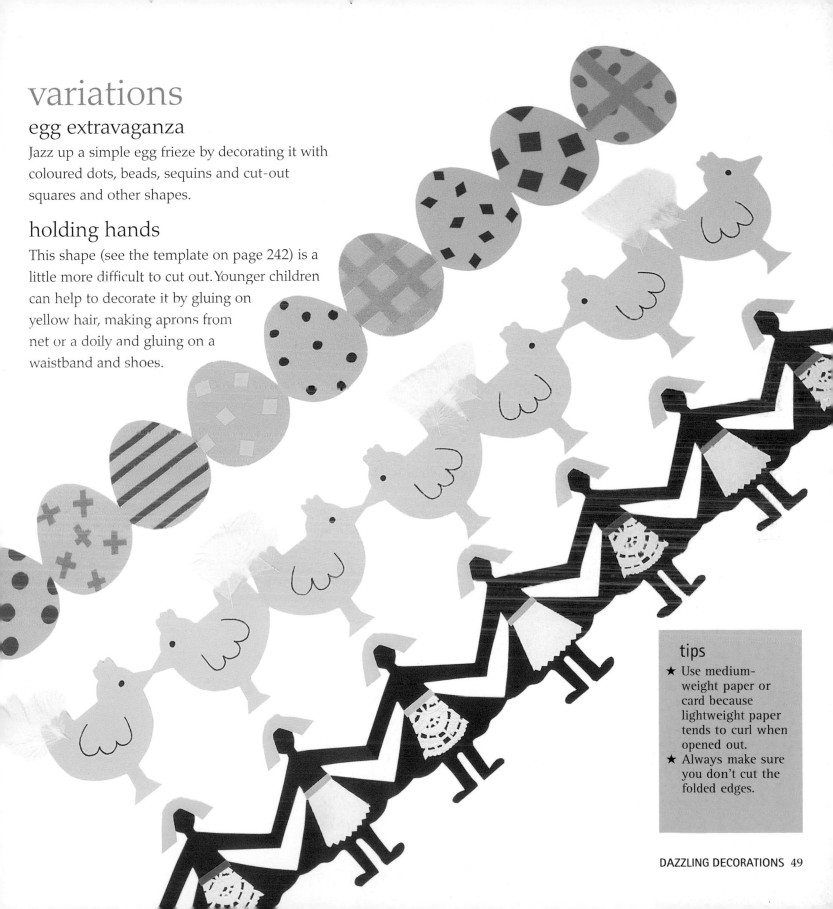

tips

★ Use medium-
weight paper or
card because
lightweight paper
tends to curl when
opened out.
★ Always make sure
you don't cut the
folded edges.

**time needed
1 hour**

what you need

Ruler

Pencil

Scissors

Yellow crepe paper

All-purpose household
glue

4 green bendy plastic
drinking straws

Mid-green paper

Clear sticky tape

Light green tissue paper

Organza ribbon

paper daffodils

ages 6–8 years

This delightful bouquet of paper daffodils is an ideal springtime gift. As a finishing touch, present the flowers with some vibrant green paper leaves wrapped in colourful tissue paper.

1 For each flower trumpet cut a 6 x 4.5 cm (2½ x 1¾ in) rectangle of yellow crepe paper, cutting the short edges parallel with the lines on the paper. Gently stretch one long edge between your fingers.

2 Glue the short edges together to form a trumpet-shaped tube. Cut off the top of a green bendy drinking straw 2 cm (¾ in) above the bend. Dab glue inside the bottom of the trumpet. Slip the top of the straw into the trumpet and squeeze the bottom of it around the straw.

3 Trace the petal template on page 247 then transfer the design six times onto the yellow crepe paper, matching the arrow on the template to the direction of the lines on the paper. Cut out the petals. Glue the bottom of three petals around the trumpet. Glue the other petals in the gaps. Leave the glue to dry, then open out the petals. Bend the top of the straw 'stalk' forward.

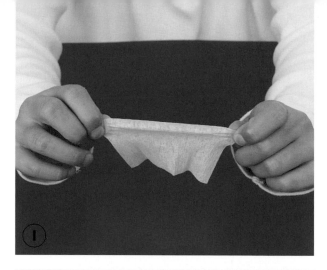

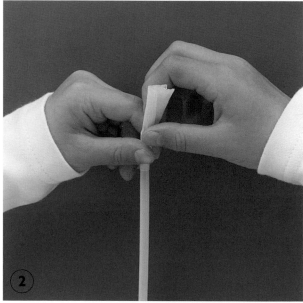

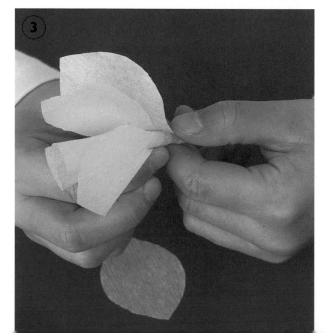

(4) Using the leaf template on page 247, cut a leaf from the mid-green paper. Fold the leaf along the centre, then open it out flat again. Gently pull the tip of the leaf between thumb and finger to curve the leaf tip backward.

5 Repeat the steps to make four daffodils and four leaves. To make a pretty bouquet, bunch the daffodils and leaves together and bind them in position with clear sticky tape.

6 Wrap the flowers and leaves in a piece of light green tissue paper. Tie this gift wrap in place with a length of organza ribbon.

tip
★ Gently push your thumb into the crepe paper trumpet to open out the shape.

variations

purple fringed flower

Cut a 6 x 4 cm (2½ x 1½ in) rectangle of pale pink crepe paper. Cut one long edge into a fringe. Glue the other long edge around the top of the straw. Make six petals from purple crepe paper and glue them around the straw.

cerise feather flower

Glue yellow feathers into the top of a straw. Make six petals from bright pink crepe paper and glue them around the straw.

fringed feather flower

Glue green feathers into the top of a straw. Cut a 45 x 6 cm (18 x 2½ in) strip of pale pink crepe paper. Cut one long edge into a fringe. Glue the other long edge around the top of the straw.

hanging chickens

ages 2–6 years

These Easter chicks look very sweet hanging at a window or from a twig or plant. Make them in different sizes either by cutting them out of paper or using polystyrene eggs. Polystyrene eggs are great for younger children to paint and pipe cleaners can be pushed into them easily to make features, legs and tails. Beads, sequins and coloured feathers are ideal for further decorations.

1 Push a wooden skewer into the base of the egg, then paint the egg bright yellow, holding onto the skewer. Anchor the skewer until the paint has dried.

2 When dry, cut up coloured pipe cleaners: two blue bits for the eyes, orange for the beak and comb, brown and black stripes for the legs and tail. Push the eyes, beak and comb into position.

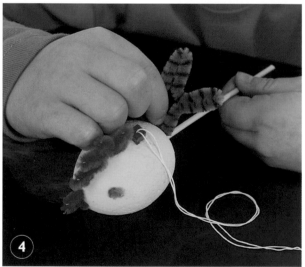

3 Thread a bead onto a length of elastic or string, securing it with a knot. Make a hole in the top centre of the egg with a skewer and glue the bead into it.

4 Push in pipe cleaners for the legs and tail.

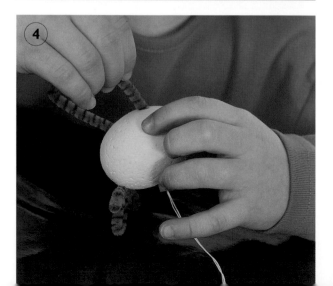

30

time needed
30 minutes

what you need

Polystyrene egg

Wooden skewer

Paint

Brush

Scissors

Coloured pipe cleaners

Glue

Elastic

Bead

variations

changing chicks

To change the look, paint polystyrene eggs in different colours and decorate with feathers and beads. Hang on Easter twigs.

paper chicks

Make paper chicks by drawing your own template. Decorate them with feathers, use threaded beads for the legs or simply colour them with crayons.

tips

★ Dab a dot of glue onto pipe cleaners to prevent them from falling out of the polystyrene egg.
★ Keep sharp skewers away from young children: remove them once the paint has dried.

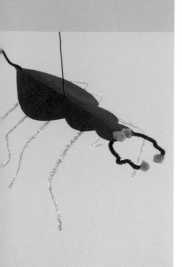

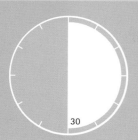

**time needed
30 minutes**

what you need

Black paper

White pencil

Scissors

Silver and black pipe
cleaners

Sticky tape

Black cotton

Orange wool or beads
for eyes

giant insect

ages 2–6 years

Hanging spiders and insects, ghosts,
eyeballs and all the horrible things you
can think of will all add to a Halloween
party atmosphere. Simple cut-outs of
giant creepy-crawlies and paper ghosts
require little skill to make. The eyeballs
may take a little longer, but whatever
you choose to make, all ages will have
plenty of fun.

(**1**) Fold a piece of black paper in half. Using
the template on page 243, draw half a beetle
shape onto the paper with a white pencil and
cut out the shape with scissors.

(**2**) Place four silver pipe cleaners into position
on the underside of the back for the legs and a
black one for the feelers. Stick them down with
tape. Make a small hole in the centre of the
back and thread through a length of black
cotton. Tie it in a knot to secure.

(**3**) Make a small hole at the tail end of the
beetle and thread through a piece of black pipe
cleaner. Bend the legs to make the beetle stand
up. Stick on orange wool or beads for the eyes
and the ends of the feelers.

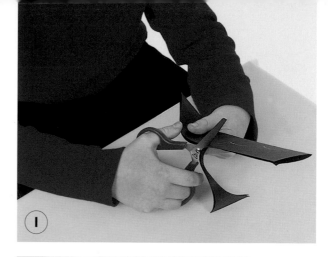

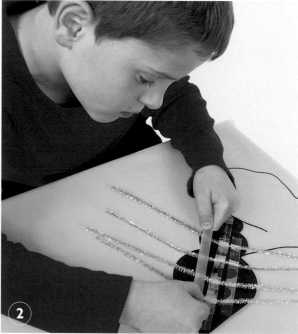

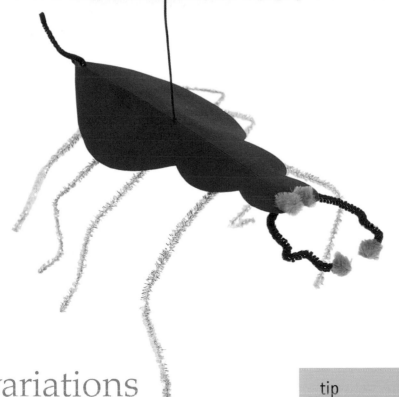

variations

dangling eyeballs

Make a ghoulish hanging with polystyrene balls decorated as eyeballs. Pierce a hole in the polystyrene ball, apply some glue to the hole and thread in a piece of cord. Leave to dry before using.

incey-wincey spiders

Black cut-out spiders threaded onto ribbon will look especially creepy at a window.

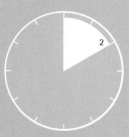

chopstick wind chimes

ages 6–7 years

Let these stripey wind chimes tinkle in the breeze by hanging them in the garden or indoors by an open window.

(1) Paint six chopsticks in stripes using shades of blue, turquoise, purple and lilac. Wash and dry the paintbrush between each colour. Insert the chopsticks into a piece of plastic clay to dry.

(2) Cut six equal lengths of narrow braid. Tie one length around the top of each chopstick. Fix them in place with a dab of glue.

3   Use the large needle to make six holes around the edge of the plastic lid. (An adult might like to help at this stage.)

(4) Thread the braid from one chopstick up through one hole. Knot the braid on top of the lid. Fix all the chopsticks to the lid, making sure that they hang down at the same level.

5   Make a hole in the centre of the lid with the needle. To hang the chimes, thread another length of narrow braid through the hole and knot it beneath the lid.

**time needed
2 hours**

what you need

6 chopsticks

Blue, turquoise, purple and lilac acrylic paint

Medium paintbrush

Plastic clay

Narrow braid

Scissors

PVA glue

Large needle

Plastic lid from snack tube

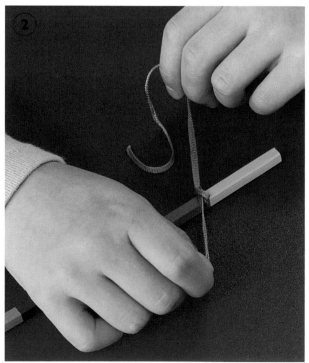

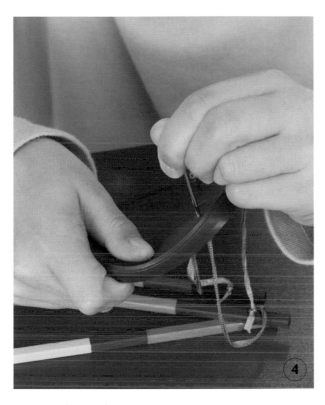

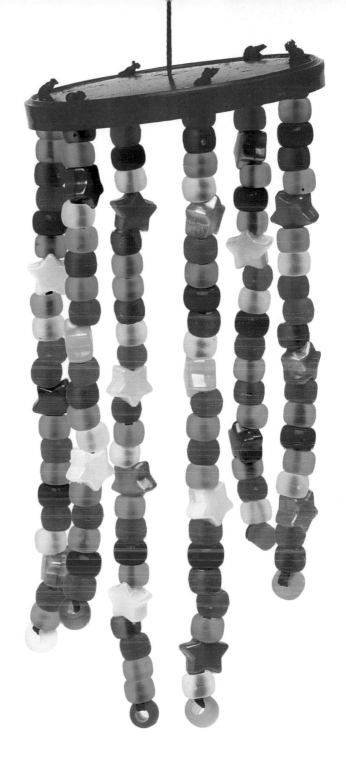

variation
bead mobile

Cut six equal lengths of ribbon. Thread a bead onto the centre of each length. Thread both ends through multicoloured beads (keep the colours random). Punch six holes around the edge of a plastic snack tube top and thread both ends of the ribbons through each hole, knotting as before. Suspend from a ribbon fixed to a hole in the centre of the lid, as before.

tip
★ Dab glue on the knots to hold them in place.

carved pumpkins

age 5–6 years

Halloween wouldn't be complete without a carved pumpkin face to put on your doorstep with a lighted candle inside. Look out for the smaller varieties of squashes and gourds as well: these take very little time to cut out and make pretty lanterns on Halloween night or for a party.

(1) Cut the top off the pumpkin and scoop out the flesh with a spoon. Scrape out as much flesh from the sides of the pumpkin as you can, as the thinner it is, the easier it is to carve.

(2) Draw a scary face on the pumpkin with a black felt-tipped pen. Cut out the features with a knife (or craft knife).

(3) Make small holes in the top of the pumpkin and stick twigs in them to make hair.

**time needed
15–20 minutes**
(depending on pumpkin size)

what you need
Pumpkin
Knife (or craft knife)
Spoon
Black felt-tipped pen
Twigs

CAUTION!

Be very careful with lighted candles. Do not leave them burning unattended and remember not to put the pumpkin top on when a candle is lit otherwise it will start cooking and burn.

variations

different colours

Squashes and gourds of varying sizes and colours can be decorated with simple holes made with an apple corer or a skewer.

different shapes

Draw star and flower shapes on a pumpkin with a black felt-tipped pen and cut them out with a craft knife.

③

tip
★ Save the leftover pumpkin seeds to roast and eat.

**time needed
1 hour**

what you need

Cardboard roll, about
   10 cm (4 in) long

Poster paints and brush

Green paper

Pencil

Plate

Scissors

Stapler (or sticky tape)

Coloured tissue paper

Stick glue

Sweets (or small treat)

festive trees

ages 2–6 years

These bright colourful tree gifts are ideal for a party, Harvest Festival celebration or Thanksgiving dinner. The simple cones can be decorated according to your chosen theme and the bases filled with sweets or a small treat.

1 Paint the cardboard roll green, then when it is dry paint on brown stripes. While the paint is drying, make a semicircle on the green paper by drawing around the edge of a plate. Cut a decorative border around the edge of the circle.

2 Fold the semicircle into a cone shape, ensuring the top is pointed. Staple or tape edges together to make the tree canopy.

3 Cut several layers of tissue paper into small circles. Scrunch up contrasting coloured tissue into small balls and glue to the circle centres to make flowers. Stick the flowers on to the cone.

4 Fill the base of the tree with sweets or a small treat, seal with tissue paper, then place the cone on top.

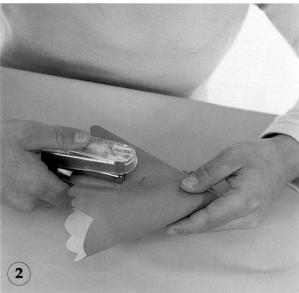

variations

snowflake and glitter tree

Make Christmassy-looking tree gifts using a tall cone from silver paper decorated with white sequins and glitter glue, or cover a red tree cone with white origami snowflakes.

fantasy tree

Create a fun tree with a zigzag edge by adding sequins, torn paper, net, or anything else that you fancy!

autumn leaf tree

Cut out leaves in autumn colours and stick them onto a brown cone for a traditional Harvest Festival look.

tips

* Cones can be given all sorts of different looks: play around with folding the paper till you get the shape you want.
* Glue the cone tops to the roll to make them more secure.
* Fill the base with sweets, then 'seal' with a ball of tissue paper.

leaves and lanterns

ages 2–6 years

Celebrate the changing of the seasons by making decorations from dried leaves and flowers. Paint them and combine them with pretty glass and plastic beads and use them to decorate your house around harvest time.

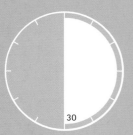

30

**time needed
30 minutes**
(plus 2 weeks to dry
leaves and lanterns first)

what you need

Leaves (or dried leaves)

Newspaper

Heavy books

Chinese lanterns
(Physalis) (or dried
Chinese lanterns)

Poster paint

Beads

Garden wire

(1) Collect attractive autumn leaves. Place them flat between eight sheets of paper (newspaper is fine) and press down with books. Leave in a warm dry place for two weeks. Allow sprigs of Chinese lanterns to dry naturally in a vase.

(2) Paint pressed leaves, choosing autumn colours. Pick off the Chinese lanterns carefully from the stems when they are dry.

(3) Thread the leaves, beads and Chinese lanterns onto the garden wire to make a hanging decoration.

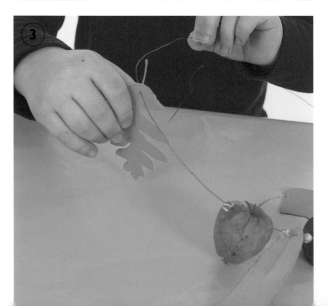

variations

hanging decorations

Thread a painted leaf and bead onto a short piece of wire and twist the wire to form a loop.

candleholder

Decorate a candleholder with painted leaves and a wire threaded with coloured beads.

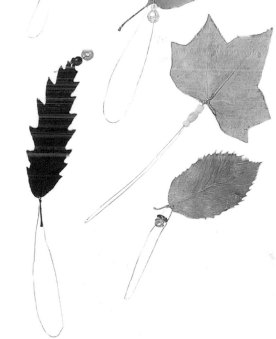

corn dolly

ages 5–6 years

These corn dollies are made from stalks and ears of grain. They are very decorative for the home and can be made by adults and children alike. Small children can participate by tying a bundle together with a pretty ribbon as a gift for a teacher or friend.

I Take a small bundle of stalks approximately 15 cm (6 in) in length. Starting a little below the top, twist two pieces of garden wire around the bundle to mark off the head.

2 Immediately below the bottom wire, separate a few strands on each side for arms. Trim these to an appropriate length, and secure each one with a little wire around the wrist area. Wrap some red wool around the wires and fasten it.

3 Make a dress by gluing lace and ribbon onto a small rectangle of fabric. Wrap the dress snugly around the doll and glue the seam down the back.

4 Glue on small dark beads for the eyes and tuck decorative heads of grain into the wool headband for additional decoration.

**time needed
30 minutes**

what you need

Dried stalks of grass, corn or grain

Garden wire

Scissors

Red wool

Glue

Lace

Ribbon

Fabric

Beads

Heads of grain

variations

boy dolly

Make a boy dolly in the same way, but separate the bundle at the bottom for legs. Make a masculine costume from little scraps of fabric and ribbon.

bundle of corn

Simply tie a few stalks together, trim the ends and decorate with ribbon and fabric. This decoration can be hung or stood on a table.

corn plait

Secure one end of a bundle to a table with tape. Plait it and twist into a shape, then tie with a ribbon and tuck in some decorate heads of grain: it's as simple as that.

heart of corn

Take two small bundles of equal length and plait them. Bend the pair into a heart shape and tie the two joins together with wire. Decorate with ribbons and a tiny bell.

tips
★ When buying bundles of grain make sure it is not too dried out as it breaks easily.
★ Even tiny scraps of fabric and ribbon can be used for decoration.

salt-dough butterfly

ages 4–6 years

Salt dough is easy to make and exciting for kids to model with. Create bright and colourful decorations for the table or give them away as gifts.

I In a mixing bowl, mix the flour and salt, then add the water gradually until the dough is firm. Knead the dough for about 10 minutes, then leave it to rest for 40 minutes at room temperature.

2 Roll out the dough to 5 mm (¼ in) thick on a pastryboard. Add a little extra flour if the dough or the rolling pin becomes too sticky.

3 Cut a butterfly shape with a cutter (or cut around a cardboard template). Use a cocktail stick to decorate with small holes. Make a hole at the base for the stick once it is cooked.

4 Place the butterfly on greaseproof paper on a baking sheet. Heat the oven to 120°C/250°F/ Gas Mark ½ and bake for about six hours, until it is hard and looks completely dried out.

5 Allow the butterfly to cool – it should be rock hard – then insert a cocktail stick into the hole with a dab of glue. Paint the butterfly with yellow poster paint and add more detail with paint in other colours.

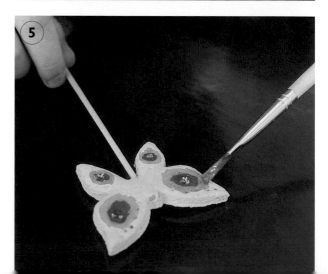

**time needed
1–2 hours**
(plus 6 hours cooking)

what you need

Mixing bowl

Spoon

2 cups plain flour

1 cup salt

1 cup tepid water

Rolling pin

Pastry board

Butterfly cutter (or cardboard template)

Cocktail stick

Baking sheet

Greaseproof paper

Glue

Poster paint (yellow and other colours)

Paint brush

tips
★ Turn the shapes regularly during cooking to keep them flat.
★ Left-over dough can be stored in a plastic bag in the refrigerator for up to five days.
★ Once decorated, you can varnish the shapes to give them a shiny protective finish, if you wish.

variations

animals and flowers

You can make all sorts of shapes using biscuit cutters, or design your own, such as the leaf here, and make cardboard templates to cut around. Decorate them using coloured paints.

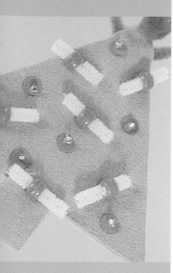

tree treats

ages 2–6 years

These special parcels make attractive Christmas tree decorations and are great mini-gifts for adults and children alike. Wrap a small present in tissue paper and place it inside the tree bag or pop in some colourful sweets or chocolates.

(1) Cut two identical Christmas tree shapes out of green felt.

(2) Place one piece of felt on top of the other and glue an orange pipe cleaner at the top of the tree between the two layers of fabric. Continue to glue around the edges then press the pieces together. Leave to dry.

(3) Glue sequins, beads and fun shapes onto the front of the tree. Place a pompom or star at the top. Leave the glue to dry.

(4) Thread a small section of pipe cleaner or wool through the holes in the beads. Dab with glue to secure.

(5) Cut a slit in the back of the tree so that the gift can be popped inside.

**time needed
20 minutes**

what you need

Scissors or pinking shears

Green felt

Assorted pipe cleaners

Sequins

Beads

PVA glue

Pompom

variations

all that glitters

If you want a sparkly tree bag, use tinsel and glitter and design a reindeer using the template on page 238.

hearts and stars

You can cut a variety of shapes in different colours, depending on the occasion, using the templates on pages 238–239.

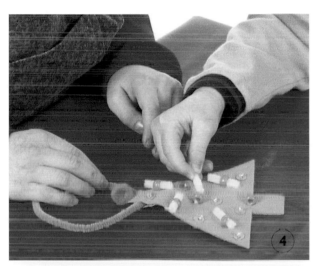

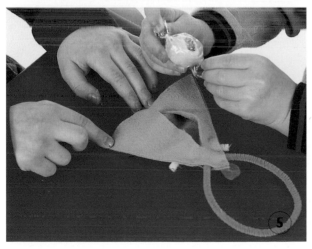

tip
★ Do not use too much glue or it will ooze out and spoil the felt.

christmas stocking

ages 5–6 years

Christmas for children isn't complete without a stocking. These unusual decorated examples can be made with adult help, but all embellishments should be left for children to do. Materials such as felt and net ensure the stockings are quite strong and should last for several Christmases to come.

1 Draw the stocking template on page 239 onto a double thickness of felt. Cut out two stocking shapes with zigzag scissors.

2 Apply glue along the edges of both stockings (except the tops). Carefully press together. While the glue is drying, make several net bows in different colours by tying a knot in a small piece of net.

3 Glue the bows and pompoms evenly all over the stocking. Cut out and stick on a hanging loop and a felt band in a contrasting colour along the top edge. Add a pompom trim below the band.

**time needed
30 minutes**

what you need

Turquoise and pink felt

Pencil

Zigzag scissors

Glue

Coloured net

Coloured pompoms

Cord or ribbon (for hanging loop)

Pompom trim

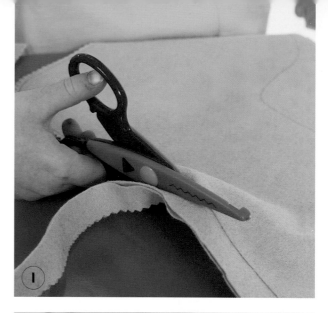

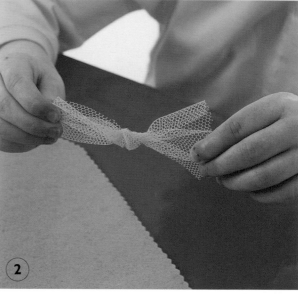

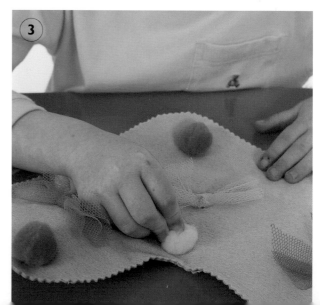

variations

cut-out shapes

For a more sophisticated look, cut a star shape out of the felt and glue contrasting coloured net to the back. Stitch both stocking shapes together with a running stitch and trim with brightly coloured beads.

see-through stocking

Stitch together stocking-shaped pieces of net with wool and trim with ribbon, plastic beads and wired-on felt. These stockings look especially effective with brightly coloured tissue-wrapped parcels inside.

tip
★ Don't fill your stocking with heavy gifts.

colourful flowers

ages 4–6 years

This cheerful selection of flower ideas for Mother's Day and Father's Day will keep children of all ages happy. Paper flowers are quick and simple to make. They can be glued onto a straw with a paper leaf and given with a gift, or made into a colourful bunch and arranged in a pot to be the gift itself.

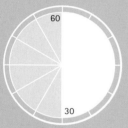

**time needed
30–60 minutes**

what you need

Green and yellow paper

Pencil

Scissors

Hole punch

Straw

Stick glue

Purple tissue paper

Ribbon

(1) Draw a leaf-shape on some green paper (fold the paper over several times to make several leaves at a time). Cut out the leaf. Punch a hole through the centre of the leaf and thread onto a straw. Stick the leaf to the straw with a dab of glue.

(2) Cut three layers of purple tissue paper into a flower shape and punch a hole through the centre. Cut a small rectangle of yellow paper for the flower centre.

(3) Thread the flower shapes onto the end of the straw. Dab some glue onto the yellow centre and stick it to the top of the straw.

4 Tie a ribbon around the straw and use on its own or pop it into a pot with a selection of other paper flowers.

variations

floral cards

Paper flowers glued to a card or placed in the fold look very effective, yet are simple to make.

flower pots

Flower pots can be made from recycled yoghurt or plastic cups. Simply paint them or cover them with paper and fill with a gift or a bunch of flowers.

tips

★ Cut several layers of tissue or paper circles at a time and make a decorative edge.
★ You may need to use a dab of glue when threading flowers and leaves onto the straws. Remember that PVA-glue will dissolve the tissue paper.

folding crocodile

ages 2–6 years

Folding decorations on sticks are fun for all ages to make. They are simply strips of paper made into creatures, insects or shapes, coloured in with crayons or felt-tipped pens and attached to wooden sticks. Adding ribbons makes them look especially festive. Pop them into a container as a decoration, play with them or use them to wave instead of a traditional flag at a festival.

I Draw a rough outline of a crocodile: a long oblong with a pair of bulging eyes at one end and tapering tail at the other end. Make the top of the back a bold zigzag. Cut out the crocodile shape.

2 Draw in the eyes, mouth and nostril with a marker pen. Draw stripes down the length of the body and colour them in using different coloured felt-tipped pens.

3 Leaving the head and tail flat, fold the middle body section concertina-style.

4 Tape two wooden sticks to the wrong side of the crocodile, one near the front and one near the back.

what you need

Paper

Pencil

Scissors

Marker pen

Felt-tipped pens

Wooden sticks

Sticky tape

76

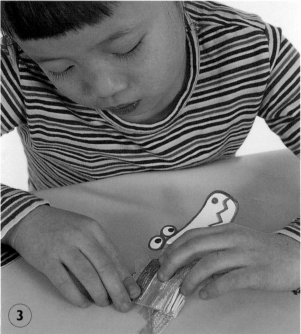

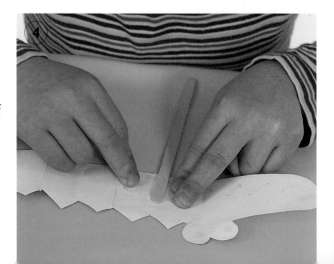

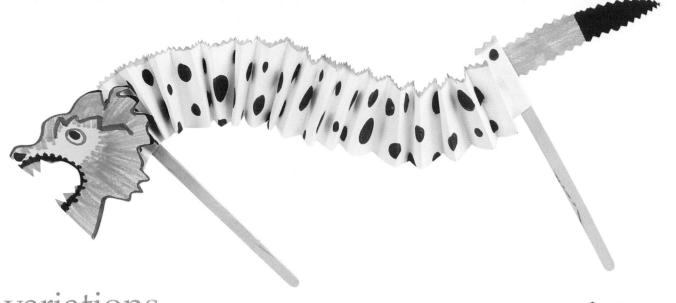

variations

mystical animals

Design your own creatures and decorate them
with glitter, coloured spots or sequins.

paper fans

Fold and colour in an elaborate fan, hanging
ribbons at the ends to jazz it up.

tips
★ For quick results, use patterned
  paper and just add the head.
★ Cut several strips of paper and
  tape them together to make a
  really long crocodile or dragon
  for two children to play with.

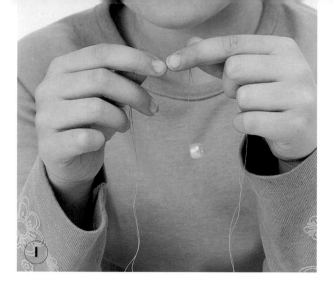

flower curtain

ages 7–8 years

This fantastic curtain of petals looks pretty hung at a window or doorway. The long 'beads' between the flowers are actually slices cut from drinking straws. As a variation, you can make a mobile by threading flower petals between stripey straw slices and crystal beads. Buy silk-look fabric flowers from florists and craft shops or very cheaply in discount homeware stores.

1. Cut the thread so it is double the length you want the bead curtain to hang plus 40 cm (16 in). (An adult should help here.) Thread one bead onto the thread. Adjust the bead so that it sits in the middle of the thread.

2. Bend the wire in half and twist the ends together to make a 'needle'. Thread both ends of the thread through the needle.

3. Cut the drinking straws into slices 5 cm (2 in) in length. Thread one slice onto the thread.

4. Pull apart the silk flowers, separating them into separate blooms. Each one should have a tiny hole for threading at the centre. Thread two flowers onto the thread.

**time needed
1½ hours**

what you need

Ruler

Scissors

Strong thread

Coloured plastic beads

15 cm (6 in) thin wire

Plastic drinking straws

Fabric flowers

Wooden batten

Acrylic paint to complement the flowers

Large paintbrush

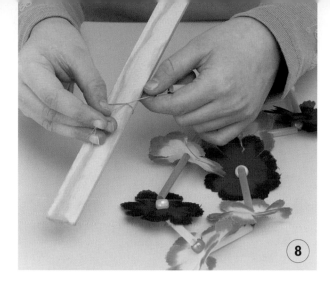

5 Thread on a bead. Continue threading on straw slices, flowers and beads until you have filled the thread. Make sure you leave enough thread at the top to tie around the batten.

6 Cut more thread and make as many flower strings as you require.

7 Paint the wooden batten in a shade that complements the flowers, and leave to dry.

8 Tie one end of each flower string to the batten, spaced at equal distances apart. To suspend, screw the batten into the window frame or hang it on a hook placed each side of the window.

tip
★ Glue the threads at the top of each flower string to the back of the curtain batten to keep them secure.

variation
flower mobile

Make up flower strings as before, then tie them to the ends of two mobile wires. Tie the wires together at the centre to form a cross. Hang the mobile on a length of strong thread, threading it with a few petals and beads.

painted flags

ages 2–6 years

Handmade paper flags, chains and hanging decorations make a colourful display for any carnival. Once the paper has been decorated, it can be cut into all sorts of shapes and sizes and will look much more interesting than anything you can buy. This brilliant project is extremely messy, so it's best done outside in the garden on a fine day.

(1) Lay sheets of paper on a protected surface (the lawn is perfect). Mix two or three colours of paint so it isn't too runny. Dip a brush into a paint and flick it across the paper. Clean the brush (or use another one) and do the same with the other colours, and on different coloured paper.

(2) Make a template of a large triangle. Once the paint is dry, draw around the template onto the coloured paper and cut out flags.

(3) Apply glue to the top edge of the flag, fold it over a length of string, and press with a finger and thumb to secure. Add the other flags to the string in the same way. Once the glue is dry, tie them up where the breeze will catch them.

**time needed
30 minutes**

what you need

Coloured paper (several colours)

Paint (several colours)

Brush (or brushes)

Card for template

Pencil

Scissors

Glue

String

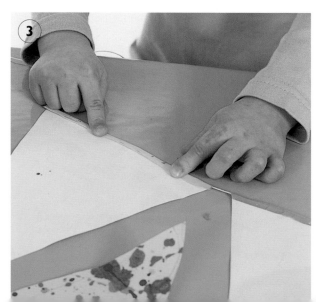

variations

paper chains

Paper chains are excellent for lots of children to make at the same time. Join them all up and see how long the chain is.

fringed flags

Cut the painted paper into small fringed rectangles as a good alternative to traditional bunting.

garden party

String up flowers with decorated centres and leaves.

tips
★ Vary the thickness of the paint for a variety of effects.
★ Always lay different coloured papers out at the same time and experiment with a selection of coloured paints.

rudolph reindeer

ages 2–6 years

Cone decorations take minutes to construct and can be made into any character you like; they are great fun for all the family to make. Give them away as gifts, use them as table decorations or simply hang them on the Christmas tree. You can decorate them with pre-cut shapes, glitter, paper and feathers as well as fabric scraps.

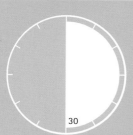

**time needed
30 minutes**

what you need

Plate

Pencil

Card (or stiff paper)

Scissors

Stapler (or sticky tape)

Black paper (or paper and crayons)

Glue

Wobbly eyes

Red pompom

1. Draw half a circle on a piece of card or stiff paper using the template on page 238 or by tracing around a plate. Carefully cut it out.

2. Make a cone shape out of the semicircle, then staple or tape it together.

3. Cut antlers out of black paper (or you could colour your own). Glue them onto the back of the cone near the top.

4. Glue the eyes onto the front.

5. Glue on a red pompom for the nose. Leave to dry.

(1)

(3)

④

⑤

variations

father christmas

Use red and white paper or card to make a traditional Santa Claus.

penguin

Glue on pompom eyes, a beak and foam feet. Make wings out of black paper and add a ribbon loop at the back so you can hang it up.

tinsel and sparkle

A home-made fairy or wise king on top of the Christmas tree will look much more special than a bought one. Glue glitter net around a cone and add either a halo or a crown.

tip
★ If you use pre-cut, self-adhesive foam or paper shapes there is no need to use glue.

festive snowman

ages 4–6 years

Made out of air-drying clay, these sparkly snowmen make excellent gifts and are good enough to keep from year to year, either as tree decorations or for a Christmas table (attach them to napkins with ribbon). Once you've made and dried the shapes, encourage everyone to get together to decorate them.

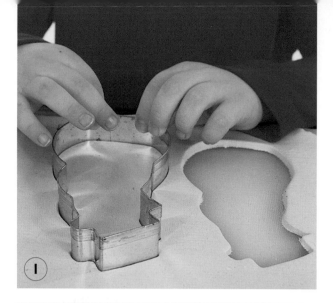

(1) Place the clay on a pastry board and roll it out to a thickness of 3 mm (⅛ in). Smooth lightly with water to keep the clay flat. If you have a snowman cutter, use it to cut out the shape, or cut around your own cardboard template with a knife. Make a small hole in the hat to thread ribbon through.

2 Leave the snowman to dry overnight, turning to keep it flat.

(3) If the clay is not white, paint it with white poster paint. Allow to dry, then put glue on the hat and sprinkle on the silver glitter. Carefully draw on a face and scarf.

(4) Use the red glitter for the scarf, and glue on a bead for the nose. Finally, thread a red ribbon through the hole in the hat and fasten it to make a hanging loop.

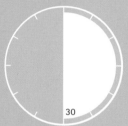

time needed
30 minutes
(plus overnight to dry)

what you need

Air-drying clay
Pastry board
Rolling pin
Snowman cutter (or cardboard template)
White poster paint
Silver and red glitter
Glue
Felt-tipped pens
Bead
Red ribbon

variations

glittering stars

Make star decorations in the same way as the snowman. You can use glitter glue instead of sprinkling glitter onto the glued surface.

beads and baubles

In fact, all sorts of painted decorations with beads and sequins glued on are quick to make. Don't forget to make holes through the clay before it dries with a pin for hanging loops, or to hang beads on the decorations.

tips

★ Try to buy white clay so that you don't have to paint it.
★ Keep clay airtight after use for future projects.
★ The painted decorations can be painted with watered-down PVA glue to give extra protection before decorating with sequins and beads.

3-D paper decoration

ages 2–6 yearss

Paper decorations look so attractive hanging at the window or on a tree. Three-dimensional ones are particularly effective hanging where they will be seen from all sides. An alternative to these three-dimensional stars is snowflakes made out of origami paper. It's always fun to unfold a snowflake and such a surprise to see how it looks!

1

(**1**) Fold a sheet of coloured card in half. Draw a star on it using the template on page 238. Cut around it to get two stars. Decorate both stars with glitter glue.

(**2**) Cut one star from a point to its centre. Make a cut in the other star from between two points to its centre. Align the cuts and slide the stars together to make a three-dimensional shape. Pierce a small hole through the point where the two stars meet and thread the cord through to make a hanging loop.

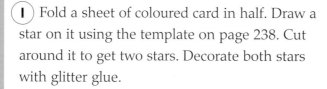

**time needed
30 minutes**

what you need

Coloured card (or thick paper)

Pencil

Scissors

Glitter glue

Pin

Cord

2

variations

different shapes

You can make angels, Christmas trees or baubles. Decorate them with stars and glitter or use two different coloured papers.

origami snowflakes

Fold a square piece of paper in half, then quarters and then into a triangle. Draw a pattern along both folded edges and then carefully cut out the snowflake shape. Unfold, flatten out and peg onto a cord.

tip
★ Three-dimensional decorations need heavy paper or thin card, or they will curl up. Snowflakes need thin paper such as origami or tissue paper, or they are too difficult to cut out.

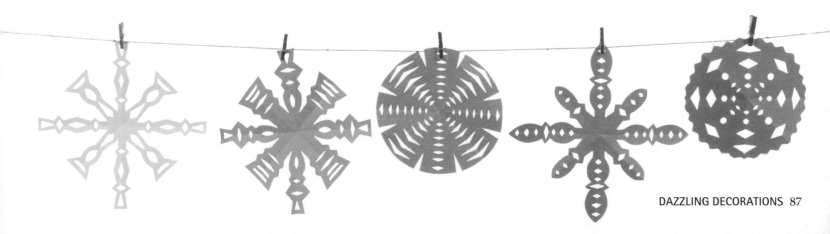

paper spiral decoration

ages 5–6 years

These festive paper hangings can be used indoors and out. The tissue paper flags look even prettier when there is a gentle breeze blowing. Inexpensive and quick to make, they can look simple or elaborate and, with parental help for very young children, a lot can be achieved in very short time!

(1) Use a plate to draw a circle on coloured paper. Cut it out. Draw a spiral shape inside the circle and cut it out.

(2) Fold pieces of coloured tissue paper several times. Draw on and cut out several pointed flag-shapes. Attach these around the spiral using glitter stickers at even intervals.

(3) Make a small hole at the top of spiral decoration (the centre of the circle) with a pin and thread through a ribbon to hang it with. Knot to secure.

time needed
20 minutes

what you need

Plate

Coloured paper

Pencil

Scissors

Coloured tissue paper

Glitter stickers

Pin

Ribbon

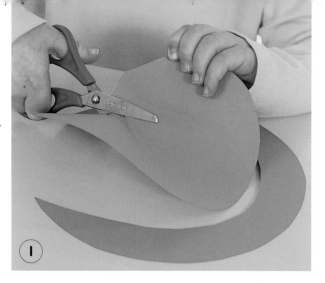

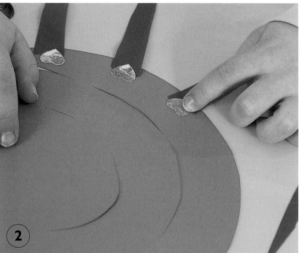

variations

chinese lanterns

Fold a piece of paper in half lengthways. Make cuts at broad intervals along the fold, leaving the top and bottom edges uncut. Unfold the paper and tape the shorter ends together. Push into shape so it resembles a lantern and stick or staple on a handle.

tissue flags

Fold a piece of tissue paper into four and cut out different patterns. Unfold and glue top edge over a ribbon to make a hanging banner. Don't forget to use stick glue.

tips

★ Cut out several decorations at a time, for quick results.
★ Mix coloured foils and gold, silver and bronze tissue paper with plain colours for a sparkly finish.

potato
people

ages 3–6 years

This is a fun idea for a party or even to take as your gift for the Harvest Festival. Before raiding the refrigerator for fruit and vegetables make sure you ask first, then use whatever you can find – you will be amazed how many different faces you can make!

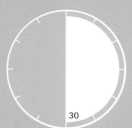

**time needed
30 minutes**

what you need

Cocktail sticks

Scissors

Knife

Large potato

2 Kumquats

Baby sweetcorn

2 Blueberries

Radish

2 Blueberries

2 Mangetout

Sprouting broccoli or
  cabbage

2 Mangetout

(1) Push cocktail sticks into all the vegetables so you can stick them in the potato. Cut the cocktail sticks in half if they are too long. First press two kumquats into the potato to make feet.

(2) Cut a piece of corn to use for a nose. Then stick two blueberries above the nose for eyes and cut a radish for the mouth.

3 Place a mangetout on each side of the potato for earrings.

(4) Add a few leaves of sprouting broccoli or cabbage for the hair and top it off with a broccoli floret hat.

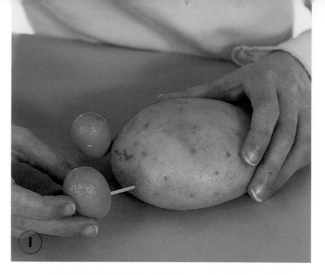

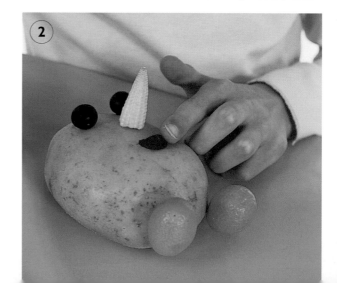

variations

- Give a sweet potato green feet made from spring onion stalks. Add radish eyes and a blueberry nose and top with kale hair and a kumquat and bean hat.

- Add rings of carrot for legs to a large baking potato. Cut out mangetout lips, radish eyes and an onion nose. Make a hat with mushroom and onion and secure it to kale hair.

- Create a colourful character out of a red potato with courgette feet, a carrot nose, corn eyes and blueberry ears. An onion-stalk hat can be decorated with aubergine.

tips
★ Only make these characters immediately before they are needed – keep them outside and spray with water to keep fresh.
★ Use a cut-down skewer at the back of the potato to help it stand up.

peg doll

ages 4–6 years

A selection of national dolls made out of pegs shows how original and different costumes from other countries can look, using only a few scraps of lace, wool and ribbon. A monk's simple habit made from felt and string is a great contrast to an exotic Indian outfit made from bright ribbons. These festive dolls are entertaining and educational for all ages.

(**1**) Paint a wooden peg all over with dark brown poster paint.

(**2**) Tie a brown pipe cleaner around the peg below the face to make arms. Trim to the right length. Paint a simple face onto the front of the peg: two blue dots for eyes and a red dot for a nose and a mouth.

(**3**) Glue one end of a green ribbon to the peg and wrap it around the body sari-style, leaving the arms protruding on either side. Glue the other end of the ribbon at the back and attach a gold sash or small tassel, if you wish. Glue a tiny roll of brightly coloured ribbon to the head as a turban.

**time needed
30 minutes**

what you need

Old-fashioned wooden peg

Poster paint (brown, blue and red)

Brush

Brown pipe cleaner

Scissors

Glue

Coloured ribbons

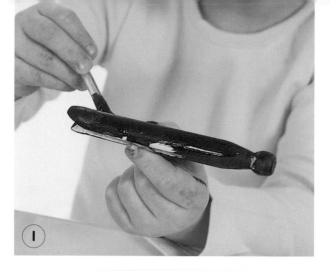

variations

- Make an oriental doll using patterned paper or ribbon and black wool hair cut in a bob. Make a plait of wool for an Indian doll's hair and paint on a face with poster paint.

- Find out about festivals around the world and make dolls to represent the people of those countries. See how many different dolls you can make.

tips
★ Raid your scrap basket for this project and it won't cost a penny.
★ If you can't find wooden pegs, use wooden lolly sticks instead.

make it, wear it

loved-up T-shirt

ages 5–6 years

Help your loved ones to wear their hearts on their chests by stencilling them a heart T-shirt. Any design looks stunning in silver textile paint, and you only have to iron it to fix the paint. The stencil can be used several times.

(**1**) Make a stencil using the heart template on page 241 or by drawing half a heart on a folded piece of paper and cutting it out with scissors.

(**2**) Iron the T-shirt flat. Place a piece of paper inside the T-shirt (to protect the back). Position the heart stencil on the front of the T-shirt and tape it down. Paint on the stencil paint gently with short dabs.

(**3**) Remove the stencil when the paint is dry (if it dries flat you can use the stencil again). Iron to fix the paint, following the manufacturer's instructions.

**time needed
30 minutes**

what you need
Paper
Pencil
Scissors
T-shirt
Iron
Sticky tape
Stencil paint
Brush

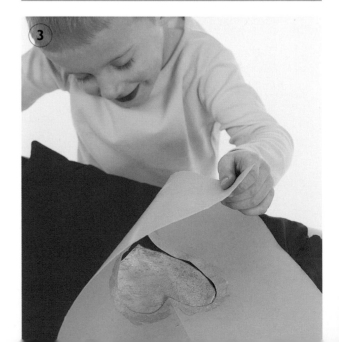

variations

love-lights

Add a touch of sparkle to your stencilled heart
by using glitter fabric glue and heart diamantés.

sweetheart bag

Stencil a silver heart onto a piece of felt. Glue
around the edges onto another piece of felt
the same size and add glitter, sequins and a
ribbon handle.

star socks

Make a pretty pair of socks look extra special by
adding a tiny stencilled star motif embellished
with glitter glue.

tip
★ Always test the stencil out first
on a spare piece of fabric.

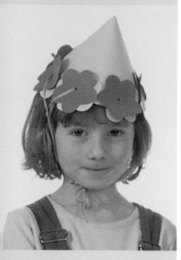

flowery bonnet

ages 2–6 years

A decorative hat is a must for all Easter celebrations. Conjure up something bright and cheerful by using scraps of paper, zigzag scissors, feathers, beads and ribbons. It was once customary to wear something new on Easter Sunday, so why not make a hat for each member of the family?

**time needed
30 minutes**

what you need

Pencil

Yellow paper

Large plate

Scissors

Pink and purple paper
(or flower-shaped
self-stick notes)

Hole punch

Stapler

Ribbon

(**1**) Draw a circle on yellow paper, using a large plate to draw around. Cut out the circle and then cut a line into the centre of the circle. Fold the paper round to make a conical hat. Check it on the child (or adult) for head size, then staple the sides together.

2   Make six to eight large pink paper flowers and the same number out of purple paper. Use flower-shaped self-stick notes, if you can find them.

(**3**) Glue a pink flower on top of a purple one, making sure the petals don't overlap completely. Punch a hole through the centre of each flower. Attach pairs of flower around the brim of the hat.

(**4**) Thread a ribbon through a flower on each side of the hat, to go under the chin, and secure with a knot.

98

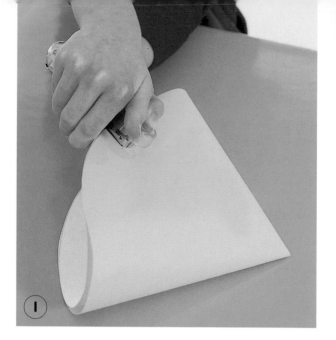

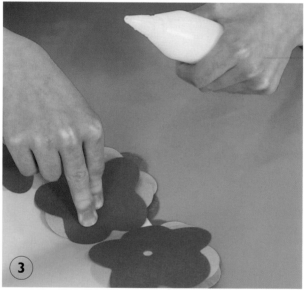

variations

folded bonnet

The folded bonnet has a cut decorative edge top and bottom with cut circles threaded with ribbon and knotted on each side. Decorate with pre-cut flower shapes or cut your own – the bonnet can be tied around the head or secured with hair grips.

hat bands

A broad strip of coloured paper decorated with flowers and feathers makes a quick stylish hat. Either staple the band together neatly overlapping or cross over at the front. Cut a circle into a spiral and stick only one end onto the band so the other hangs away from the hat.

tip
★ Use a small plate as a template for a small hat or a larger plate for a larger bonnet.

scary skeleton

ages 5–6

Glow-in-the-dark paint and glitter work brilliantly for a trick or treat party, or whenever the lights are turned out. The paint and sparkle goes a long way so, it's ideal for several friends to have a go at creating decorations or their own scary skeleton T-shirt.

(1) Draw bone shapes on white paper: ten sausages for ribs, seven rough circles for back vertebrae and elbows, and four traditional cylinders with a bulb at each end for the arms. Cut them out and position them on the front of the T-shirt. Tape them down so they don't move. Draw around the shapes with a white pencil.

(2) Remove the sticky tape and paper bones and place a piece of paper inside the T-shirt to make sure the paint doesn't go through to the back of the fabric. Paint the bone shapes with white fabric paint.

(3) When the paint is completely dry (leave it overnight to be sure), lightly paint over the bones with glow-in-the-dark paint. Add a second coat of paint for an even better effect if you wish.

**time needed
1–2 hours**
(plus overnight to dry)

what you need

White paper

Pencils (ordinary and white)

Scissors

Black T-shirt (preferably long-sleeved)

Sticky tape

White fabric paint

Paint brush

Glow-in-the-dark paint

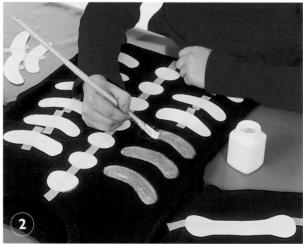

variations

night sky

Glittery glow-in-the-dark stars, moons and planets (use the templates on pages 238 and 244), are very effective party decorations. Simply fasten them on a wall or window with sticky tape or hang them from a piece of cord.

party invitations

Make a party invitation by sticking your motif to a card and complete it with glow-in-the-dark writing. Give clear instructions on the envelope that it must be opened in the dark.

tip

★ Use low-adhesive tape for sticking decorations to walls so that no damage occurs.

time needed
30 minutes

what you need
Black paper
Pencil
42 cm (17 in) string
Drawing pin
Scissors
Glitter
Glue

wizard's hat

ages 4–6 years

A ghoulish costume is essential for Halloween. If you haven't much time, a glittering wizard's hat and a simple black cloak should do the trick.

I Mark the centre of the black paper with a pencil. Tie the string to the pencil and pin the other end of the string to the centre of the paper with a drawing pin. Hold the pin in place with your thumb and, keeping the string taut, draw a half circle. Cut out the shape.

2 Make a cone with the paper and try it on your child's head for size. Staple the sides together.

3 Draw different sized stars onto black paper with a white pencil using the templates on page 238. Cut out the star shapes, spread them with glue and sprinkle with plenty of glitter.

4 Glue your glitter star shapes evenly all over the wizard's hat.

variations

bug bangles

Plastic creepy-crawly insects are perfect to make bangles and necklaces with. Just twist them on to sparkly pipe cleaners. They only take seconds to make and will be greatly admired on the night.

little devil

Furry devil head bands are just the thing for younger children.

tip

★ Buy a big bag of plastic bugs: friends and family will love making things with them!

skull mask

ages 4–6 years

Paper plates are an ideal surface for children to decorate and they make excellent masks. Let your imagination run wild and create a unique Halloween mask for your fancy dress costume: perhaps a scary monster, witch's cat or a pumpkin face.

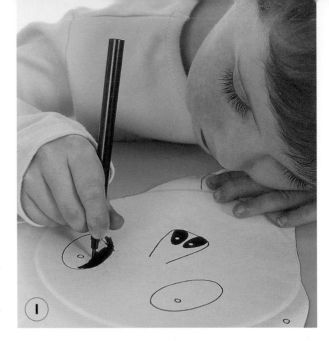

1 Draw a skull with hollow cheeks on a paper plate. Hold the face up to your own and get someone to mark where the holes for the eyes and nose should be. Also mark small holes on either side for the elastic cord. Using a black felt-tipped pen, shade in the eyes, nose and mouth.

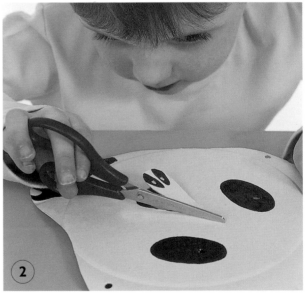

2 Cut around the nose and pierce the eyes (if scissors are too big, ask an adult to help you do this with a knife). Use a hole punch to open the holes at the side of the mask for elastic to go through.

3 Make the top part of the jaw from a piece of the embossed edge of the paper plate that you have cut away. Glue it in place above the mouth. Knot one end of the elastic cord and thread it through a hole, check it for size and knot the other end through the second hole.

10

30

**time needed
10–30 minutes**

what you need

White paper plate

Pencil

Scissors

Knife

Black felt-tipped pen

Elastic cord

variations

witch's cat

For a black cat, make a half mask, paint it black and add a pink paper nose and long whiskers.

scary monsters

Make pumpkin and monster masks by gluing crêpe paper over a plate and sticking on scrunched up bits for warts. Decorate the masks in any sludgy colour you like with felt-tipped pens and glitter glue. (Remember to use stick glue for crêpe paper.)

tip

★ Choose lightweight paper plates as they are easier to handle and wear.

feathered headband

ages 4–6 years

Why not make a headband for every member of the family to wear for a themed Thanksgiving dinner? They will look especially good when matched with the colourful table decorations given in the variations. Feathers can be bought or made from paper, and more details added in the form of scraps of paper, ribbon and beads.

1 Mark out a strip 3 cm x 60 cm (1½ in x 24 in) on a piece of orange paper and cut it out. Stick gold rickrack braid along one long edge.

2 Make decorations from contrasting coloured circles of paper and silver paper with scrunched up tissue glued to the centre. Stick them at intervals along the band.

3 If you have some real feathers, use them. If not, you can make some out of coloured paper. Draw a long pointed oval with a stalk at one end. Cut it out, then make lots of small cuts all the way around the edge. Tape them sticking up at even intervals along the inside of the band.

4 Measure the band around the child's head, trim it to size if necessary and staple together to form the headband.

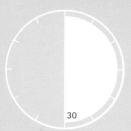

**time needed
30 minutes**

what you need

Pencil

Ruler

Coloured paper (orange and other colours)

Scissors

Rickrack braid

Silver paper

Tissue paper

Stick glue

Feathers (optional)

Sticky tape

Stapler

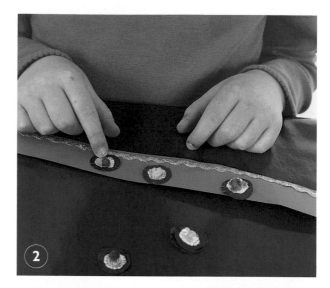

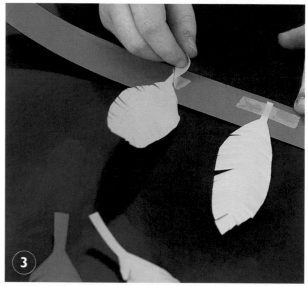

variations

placemats and napkin holders

Make placemats by simply cutting a piece of corrugated card to size, and gluing on a feather motif. For the napkin holders, cut a cardboard tube and cover with coloured paper. Add beads and feathers to decorate.

turkey place card

The turkey features strongly at Thanksgiving, so it makes a good motif for place cards. Draw a turkey, cut it out and colour it in. Stick onto a piece of folded card.

tip
★ Make different versions of the headband with tissue, ribbons and sequins. Any colourful scraps will look attractive, so feel free to experiment.

birthday bandannas

ages 5–6 years

These brightly patterned bandannas are a great idea for a children's birthday party. With special felt-tipped pens for use on fabric and stencils it doesn't take long to design a small piece of material. Younger children can participate by adding dots and lines, while you can write messages using the darker pens.

**time needed
15–30 minutes**

what you need

Cloth or handkerchief

Iron

Stencil

Coloured felt-tipped
fabric pens

1 Iron the handkerchief into quarters, then open it out and use the creases to mark where to put the stencil. Draw around the stencil with a felt-tipped fabric pen.

2 Colour in the line drawing using the felt-tipped fabric pens.

3 Iron to fix the design, following the manufacturer's instructions.

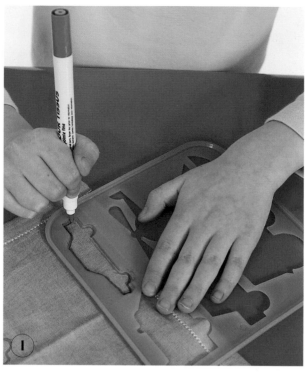

variations

fluorescent colour

Make an eye-catching border using a fish and star stencil and fluorescent felt-tipped pens. Go for a bright contrast such as simple dots of fluorescent pink on a dyed orange background.

teddy-bears' picnic

Have a bandanna party for all your teddy bears.

tips

★ Men's handkerchiefs make good sized bandannas.
★ Try dying some white hankerchiefs for a colour background.

paper crowns

ages 2–6 years

Hats made from plain or patterned tissue paper can be decorated with feathers, sequins, glitter glue and different types of paint. This easy project is fun for all ages and even very young children can share in the activity without too much mess. The great things about these hats is that you can cut out several at the same time. Have a 'party-hat party', where you let your friends decorate their own hat!

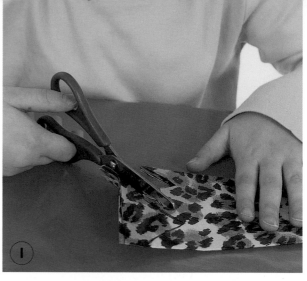

(1) Cut a length of patterned tissue paper long enough to go around your head and fold it into quarters. Mark a zigzag along the top with a felt-tipped pen and cut it out.

(2) Tape the sides of the hat together to fit around your head.

(3) Apply gold glitter glue randomly over the surface of the hat. Allow the glue to dry before you put the hat on.

**time needed
5–10 minutes**

what you need

Patterned tissue paper

Scissors

Felt-tipped pen

Sticky tape

Gold glitter glue

variations

- Look out for tissue paper in unusual colours or with unusual prints, or even reuse any that you are given.

- Cut out hats with different decorative edges. Coloured sticky tapes are a quick method of embellishing a hat.

- Glitter and sequins give a sparkle to plain tissue and feathers can be glued or stapled on. But only use lightweight sequins and feathers.

hawaiian costume

ages 5–6 years

This costume conjures up the carnival atmosphere, especially if it's made in vibrant colours. You just need a sunny day to wear it! Crêpe paper is amazingly strong, so this no-sew outfit means that children can get help to make it.

1 Measure the child's waist and the length from waist to knee. Cut out a rectangle of these dimensions in each of the coloured crêpe papers.

2 Lay the papers flat one on top of another and clip them in place. Staple them along the top edge. Unroll a length of sticky tape, sticky-side up, on a table. Carefully place the stapled edge of the papers on half of the sticky tape, then fold over the other half, pressing it down firmly along the length.

3 Cut the skirt into strips of equal width, leaving a band of at least 2.5 cm (1 in) along the top uncut.

4 Punch a hole in each end of the sticky tape, and strengthen it with a hole reinforcement. Thread a ribbon through both holes to tie the skirt on.

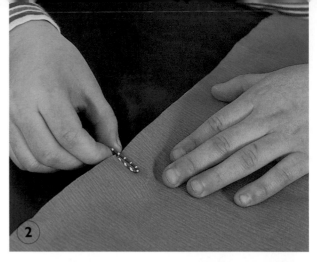

**time needed
30 minutes**

what you need

Tape measure

Crêpe paper in 4 colours (one must be yellow)

Scissors

Stapler

Wide, clear sticky tape

Hole punch

Ring reinforcements

Ribbon

variations

flowers in your hair

Make a paper flower to wear in the hair.
Try one with a contrasting centre and a cut
green leaf.

hair band

Glue some different coloured flowers onto a
hair band.

garland

Make flower garlands by threading cut-up
coloured straws and circles of coloured paper
or flower shapes alternately onto a ribbon.

glitter mask

ages 2–6 years

Masks act as a disguise, giving an air of mystery and excitement. These glittery masks can be as simple or as complicated as you wish. It's a good opportunity to use beautiful glitters, exotic feathers and an assortment of sequins and beads. Paper half-masks are especially good for young children to make and if time is short you can always decorate a bought one.

1) Fold the paper in half and draw half of your mask shape – the folded edge is the middle of your mask. Cut it out. Cut out the eyes and punch holes at the sides for the elastic cord, then reinforce them with a ring reinforcement or sticky tape.

2) Work on a surface that is easy to clean such as a plastic table cloth. Spread glue all over the mask. Sprinkle on different coloured glitters, covering the mask well. Allow to dry then shake off the excess.

3) Thread elastic through the holes at the sides of the mask. Knot securely after making sure it sits comfortably on the child's face.

30

**time needed
30 minutes**

what you need

Strong paper or card

Pencil

Scissors

Hole punch

Ring reinforcements or
  sticky tape

Glue

Coloured glitters

Elastic cord

variations

choose a theme

Why not try an insect, harlequin or exotic
eastern-looking mask. Decorate it using
feathers, stick-on sequins, glitter paint and
glitter glue.

ready-made masks

These make an instant disguise and can be
decorated in numerous exciting ways. Try glitter
stars, camouflage, zebra or leopard prints.

tips
★ Never use thin paper because it
  will tear.
★ Always strengthen the holes for
  elastic with ring reinforcements
  or sticky tape.

see-through crown

ages 2–6 years

This is surely among the best projects ever: it's very simple and quick to do, good fun for all ages, and the results are both stunning and satisfying. Using clear tape means there are endless ways of achieving a unique and imaginative festive idea.

(1) Cut out narrow strips of coloured paper. Lay them in a line about 25 cm (10 in) long on a board or table. Sprinkle glitter, silver stars and sequins over the paper strips.

(2) Place one length of tape over your decorated band of coloured strips and press it down firmly. Carefully peel it off the table and turn it over. Press on another length of tape, so the paper and decorations are sealed in a pocket of tape.

(3) Make a second strip of paper and decorations in the same way and join the pieces of tape together with more tape to form a crown. Check your child's head size before you make the join.

**time needed
10–20 minutes**

what you need

Coloured or patterned
    paper

Scissors

Ruler

Glitter

Stars

Sequins

Very wide clear
    sticky tape

variations

spangly bangle

Use leftover pieces to make into a bangle. Pre-cut shapes, sequin strips and feathers are all suitable materials.

sticky ideas

Make a photo frame or a spotty dog brooch. Cut-up pieces of decorated tape can be threaded onto wire to make a necklace.

tips

★ It is easier to make two smaller pieces for a crown rather than one long one.
★ Turn the wide tape over to make a narrow decorative strip rather than using narrow tape.

sunburst T-shirt

ages 5–6 years

Tie-dye on white fabric can produce brilliant colours and is an exciting way to brighten up old clothes or other pieces of fabric. Buy one of the tie-dye kits on the market, and all you have to do is follow the instructions.

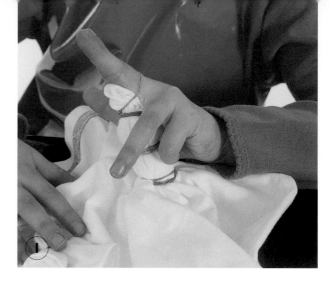

(1) Wash the T-shirt and leave it damp. To achieve a sunburst effect, pinch up the centre of the fabric at the front and add rubber bands at intervals. Also pinch a small piece of material on each sleeve and secure them with more bands.

(2) Wear rubber gloves and protect surfaces and your clothes. If using a kit, fill the bottles and paint sections according to the instructions given, either using the bottle or a dabbing on each section with a brush.

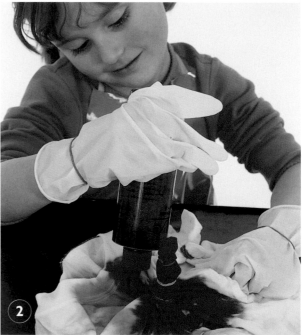

3   When you have applied the dye, place the T-shirt in a plastic bag, seal it and leave overnight for the dye to really soak in.

(4) Wearing the rubber gloves and apron, take the T-shirt out of the bag and rinse it repeatedly in cold water until the water is clear. Wash it in hot water with soap, rinse and leave to dry naturally – away from any heat.

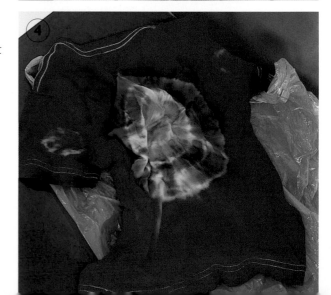

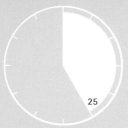

**time needed
25 minutes**
(plus overnight to soak)

what you need

T-shirt (old or new)

Tie-dye kit (or cold water dyes, bottles, paint brush and fixative)

Rubber bands

Rubber gloves

Apron

Plastic bag

118

variation

Experiment to achieve different effects. Tie off smaller and larger sections of fabric and see what effects you get from securing small buttons or stones with elastic bands

tips

★ If you can't find a tie-dye kit, use cold-water dyes with a fixative. Paint the mixed dyes on with a brush or squirt them on using plastic bottles and following the instructions in the dye pack.
★ If you want to tie-dye several pieces in the same colour, dye them in the washing machine using a machine-wash dye.

what you need

Scissors

Black and green felt

Glue

Grey wool

Glitter glue

finger puppets

ages 4–6 years

These delightful finger puppets are easy to make as there is no sewing involved and they work well on little fingers for a party, or trick or treating. There are endless Halloween characters and animals to choose from and everyone from the youngest in the family to grandparents can join in the fun of creating a spooky character.

(1) Cut out two rectangular pieces of black felt large enough to fit your finger, with a glued seam on either side. Glue three sides together, leaving the bottom open for your finger.

(2) Cut a face out of the green felt and glue it on. Cut out a black hat.

(3) Cut out black eyes, a nose and a mouth and glue them onto the face. Cut some strands of grey wool for hair and glue them into position.

4 Finally, glue the hat onto the head and decorate the face and hat with glitter glue.

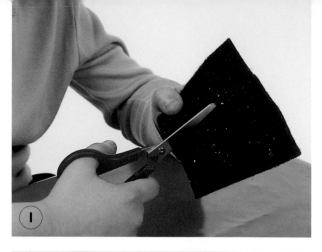

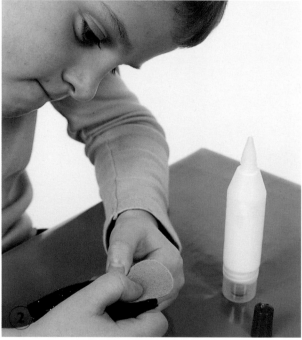

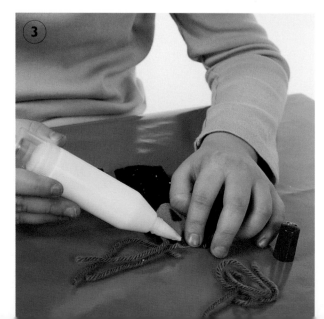

variations

monsters

Zigzag scissors make good decorative edges for
a pumpkin or skeleton. Simply make the basic
finger shape and add heads, arms and legs with
puff paint or felt-tipped pens.

mouse

This cute mouse is made from a wedge
of felt glued to form a cone. Decorate
with eyes, wool whiskers and pink
felt ears and nose.

dracula

Use red glitter felt for the body and glue on a
black cloak. Make a green felt face and decorate
with hair, eyes, eyebrows and fangs.

tip
★ Glitter felts are
particularly
effective at
Halloween.

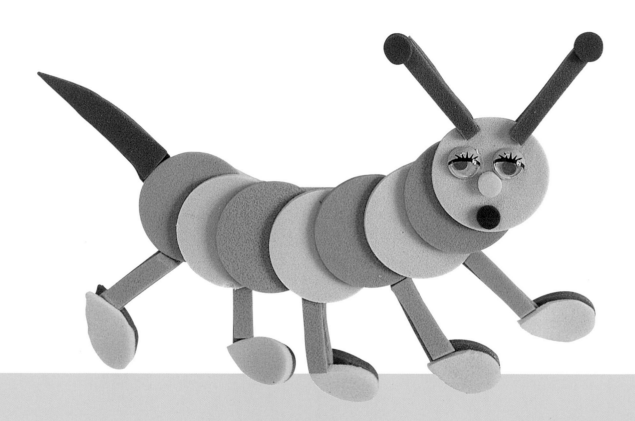

baubles, bangles and beads

**time needed
20 minutes**

what you need

30 cm (12 in) fine cord

10 coloured buttons

Key-ring

button key-ring

ages 4–6 years

We all know people who are always losing their keys. This bright, chunky key-ring is just the answer. To make it, you need to collect together lots of odd buttons in different vibrant colours to thread onto a length of fine cord.

1 Fold the fine cord in half. Make a knot about 2.5 cm (1 in) in from the fold.

2 Thread the buttons onto the cord by pushing each end of the cord through one of the holes in the buttons. Choose the buttons so you get a random selection of colours and textures.

3 When you have threaded on the last button, knot the ends of the cord together tightly beneath it. Cut off the excess cord.

4 Slip the loop of the cord onto the key-ring (an adult might need to help).

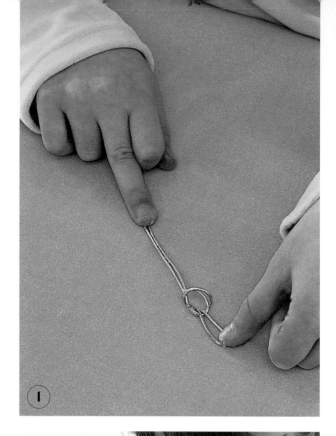

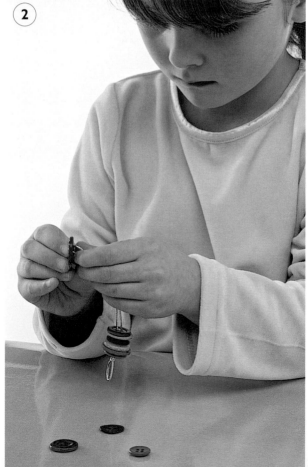

124

(3)

variations

bead key-ring

Instead of using buttons to make the key-ring, thread beads onto the cord. Make sure the beads are chunky and choose cord and beads in matching colour tones.

ribbon key-ring

Knot different-coloured ribbon directly to the key-ring. Make sure the pieces of ribbon are all about the same length and cut the ends of the ribbons at a slant.

felt flower key-ring

Trace the flower template on page 121, then transfer the design onto thin card. Cut out the shape and draw around it six times on distinct bright colours of felt or in different shades of the same colour. Cut out the flowers. Make a hole through the centre of each and thread them onto the key-ring cord as before.

tips
★ Dab the ends of the cord with glue to stop them unravelling.

time needed
15 minutes

what you need

All-purpose household
  glue

Coloured feather

Metal hair clasp

Round jewellery stones

jewelled hair clasp

ages 6–8 years

Here is a very sparkly gift for someone special, whether it's a best friend or a glamourous granny. It combines brightly-coloured feathers with deep jewel-coloured craft stones (buy them from specialist craft stores or websites). Choose dyed feathers from a craft shop or look for fallen feathers when you are out for a walk. Jewellery stones come in all sorts of shapes and colours and are especially fun to work with when you want to make gifts look really special.

(1) Glue the coloured feather so that it pokes outward on the end of the hair clasp.

(2) Glue one of the jewellery stones on top of the feather.

(3) Continue gluing jewellery stones along the length of the hair clasp until you have a look you like. Set the hair clasp aside while the glue dries.

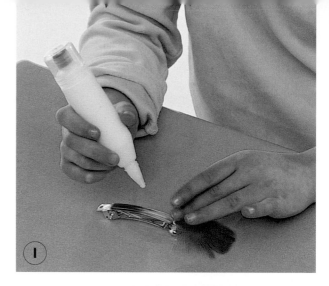

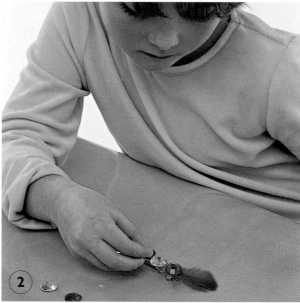

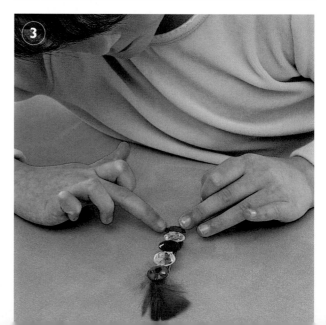

variations

use your imagination

Make all sorts of arrangements of feathers and jewellery stones on a hair clasp. Alternatively, leave out the feathers and simply glue colourful square jewellery stones in a row along the clasp. Leave to set before wearing.

tips
★ If the feathers seem too long, simply cut them to the length you want.
★ Beware of using too much glue, or it will show on the finished hair clasp.
★ Leave the glue to dry for a few hours before you handle the hair clasps.

papier-mâché choker

ages 4–6 years

It's hard to believe that this vibrant papier-mâché choker features beads made from ordinary kitchen paper! After making the beads all you have to do is paint them in bright shades and thread them onto colourful thonging.

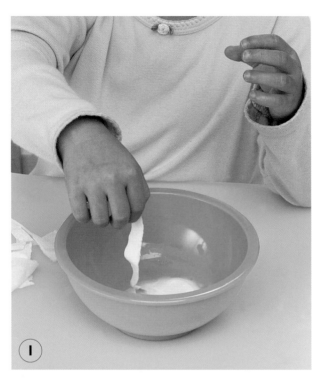

(1) Tear the sheets of paper into small pieces and leave them to soak for about an hour in a bowl of PVA glue mixed with a little water (use 1 tablespoon of water to 2 tablespoons PVA).

2 Squeeze pieces of the soaked tissue to release some of the glue and roll into seven balls about 1.5 cm (⅝ in) wide. Put the beads in a warm place for a few hours to dry.

(3) When the beads are firm, make a hole through the centre of each one using a cocktail stick. (An adult may need to help.) Gently roll the beads back into shape. Leave overnight to harden completely.

4 Slip the beads onto more cocktail sticks. Paint them blue. Insert the cocktail sticks into a piece of plastic clay and leave to dry.

(5) Paint swirls on the beads using the pink and red paint. Leave to dry.

6 Thread the beads onto the plastic thonging, knotting the thong on each side of the beads and cutting off the extra thonging.

**time needed
3 hours**
(excluding drying time)

what you need

6 sheets of kitchen paper

PVA glue

Cocktail sticks

Blue, pink and red acrylic paint

Fine paintbrush

Plastic clay

1m (3 ft) red plastic thonging

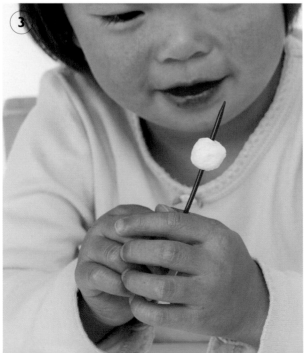

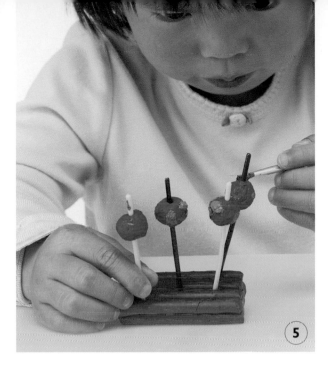

(5)

variations

bracelet

Paint eight papier-mâché beads pink and thread them onto jewellery elastic, placing a small bead between each one. Tie a knot and cut off the extra elastic.

heart pendant

Make a large papier-mâché ball, as before, then mould it into a heart shape. Make a hole through the top, allow to harden, then paint it red. Leave to dry, then apply pink glitter paint and thread onto a length of lilac cord.

tip
★ Coat the beads with clear nail varnish for protection.

foam necklace

ages 5–6 years

Foam is safe and easy to use and gives hours of pleasure to all ages. It comes in sheets or pre-cut shapes in many colours. Badges, necklaces and bracelets make ideal gifts for sisters, friends and even brothers. Some pre-cut shapes have self-adhesive backing so there is very little mess and even younger children can have a go, too.

1 Draw four flowers and five leaf shapes onto foam using the templates on page 241. Also draw 12 small squares in several different colours.

2 Cut out all the shapes. Punch a hole through one end of the leaves. Punch a hole through the centres of the flowers and squares.

3 Thread the shapes onto a piece of chenille or ribbon, alternating the flowers and leaves with the small squares. Once all the shapes are threaded, tie the ends together to make the necklace the desired length. Trim the ends if necessary.

**time needed
30 minutes**

what you need

Pencil

Coloured foam

Scissors

Hole punch

Length of chenille or ribbon

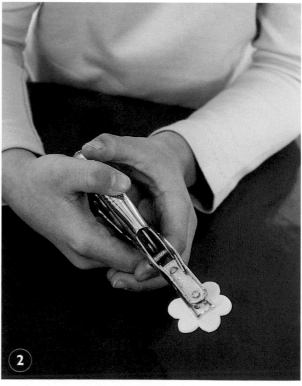

variations

easy necklace

Thread pre-cut shapes onto plastic cord, tying a knot in between each of the shapes.

bracelets

These take no time at all to make. Simply cut a foam strip (using zigzag scissors if you wish), decorate it by punching holes and tie together with strands of cut foam. You can also thread these strands through the holes.

badges

Use pre-cut shapes with plastic eyes to make a caterpillar, or be a bit more creative and cut a dog or cat shape to decorate as you please! Glue your badges to cardboard tags with a safety pins on the back, which can be bought from stationery stores.

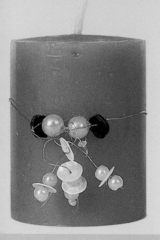

**time needed
10 minutes**

what you need

Candles

Garden wire

Scissors

Beads

Sequins

decorated candles

ages 3–6 years

Decorate these candles as a pretty gift or simply use them for a carnival celebration. Threading or gluing on beads is a very simple way of embellishing a candle. Even the youngest members of the family can contribute by helping to choose the beads and maybe by threading them. Look out for shaped sequins and unusual beads.

1 Take a small piece of wire and thread with beads and sequins, placing a large bead in the centre.

2 Thread some pearly beads onto a longer piece of wire. Pass the shorter wire through the pearls on the longer wire, leaving a small loop hanging down. Then add some red and pink sequins to the longer wire.

3 Wrap the longer wire around the candle, twisting the ends to secure them.

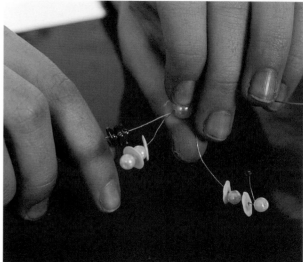

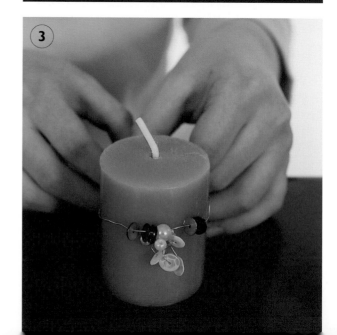

variations

sequin crazy

Hang pretty-shaped sequins from a wire or simply thread them on a wire and wrap it around the candle to give a sparkly effect.

elegant candles

Make a gorgeous gift by gluing beads and glitter stars onto tall coloured candles and placing them in a box lined with tissue paper.

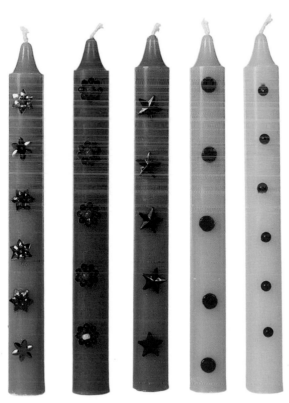

tip

★ When gluing on beads, keep the candle steady by placing tissue paper on each side. Leave to dry thoroughly or the beads fall off easily.

colourful bangles

ages 5–6 years

This fluorescent painted papier-mâché bangle will make a wonderful addition to any carnival costume. Although rather messy, this is an appealing project and the final results are well worth it.

(**1**) Tear a newsaper into small pieces and place in a bowl. Mix three parts water to one part PVA glue to cover the torn newspaper. Leave overnight.

(**2**) Squeeze the excess water out of the newspaper and add a little more PVA glue until you can begin to mould the papier-mâché.

(**3**) Find a cardboard tube wide enough for a bangle. Cut it to the size you want with a craft knife. If you need to make it smaller, cut it and tape the edges together.

(**4**) Begin placing papier-mâché pulp on the cardboard bangle. If it doesn't stick well, add more glue as you work around the bangle. Smooth the edges as you go around.

(**5**) Leave the bangle overnight to dry. Paint with white poster paint as a base colour. When dry, you can mark the pattern with a pencil first if you wish. Paint on a blue zigzag pattern, add large pink dots and finish with yellow puff paint.

45

**time needed
45 minutes**
(plus 2 nights for drying)

what you need

Newspaper

Bowl

Water

PVA glue

To decorate:

Wide cardboard tube

Craft knife

Sticky tape

Pencil

Poster paints (white, blue and pink)

Brush

Three-dimensional puff paint

Ribbon

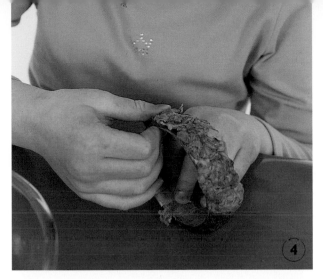

(4)

variations

papier-mâché beads

Make beads of all sizes out of papier-mâché and you can put them together to create a host of different bracelets, necklaces and earrings. Remember to pierce a hole through the wet papier-mâché before it dries overnight. Paint these bracelets and necklaces in contrasting fluorescent colours.

earrings

Use the beads to make earrings by threading through elastic cord or fishing line.

tips
★ Papier-mâché pulp will keep for up to a week, covered, in a cool place.
★ Make sure you wear old clothes and protect surfaces when working on this project.

(5)

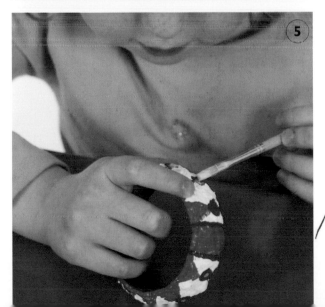

(5)

bangle bag

ages 6–8 years

This gorgeous bag has bangles for handles so it can be worn around the wrist to a special party or hung at home as a jewellery store. The bag looks best made from silky fabric: choose one to match a favourite party dress, perhaps.

(1) Cut two 16 cm (6½ in) squares of fabric with the zig-zag scissors. Pin the squares together with the right sides facing each other. Thread up the needle and, using running stitch (push the needle up from the back of the fabric to the front; pull the thread through, then push the needle from front to back a little way forward to make a straight line), sew around three of the outer edges. Start halfway down one side and finish halfway up the opposite side. Remove the pins.

(2) Fold over the side edges above the stitching and glue them down. Turn the bag right side out.

(3) Fold under 2.5 cm (1 in) of fabric on the top edge of one side of the bag. Pin a bangle under the fold. Sew below the fold to enclose the bangle, removing the pins to gather up the thread as you sew. Attach the second bangle to the other side of the bag in the same way.

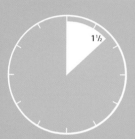

time needed
1½ hours

what you need

Tape measure

Pencil

Zig-zag scissors

20 cm (8 in) of 90 cm (36 in) wide silky fabric

Dressmaking pins

Sewing needle

Matching sewing thread

Fabric glue

2 bangles

variations

red bag

In step 3, catch in a star-shaped charm when gathering the thread by passing the needle through the loop at the top of the charm. Position the charm to sit in the centre of the gathers at the top of the bag.

orange pouch

In step 3, replace the bangles with two equal lengths of matching ribbon. Be careful not to sew in the ribbon as you sew along the fold.

> ### tip
> ★ When folding in the side edges of the bag, don't apply too much glue: it might seep through to the outside of the bag.

seed bracelet

ages 4–6 years

You can make fabulous jewellery if you collect the seeds from pumpkins and melons. Give the seeds a good wash and dry them well, then paint them and thread onto fine elastic to make this pretty bracelet. To make a necklace, all you need to do is add more seeds.

1 Paint one side of each seed lilac, aquamarine or lavender blue. Leave them to dry, then turn the seeds over and paint the other side.

2 Pierce a hole through the middle of the seeds using the thick needle. (An adult may need to help with this.)

3 Tie a knot at the end of the jewellery elastic, then thread on the seeds, alternating the colours.

4 When you have threaded on enough seeds to fit around a wrist, knot the ends of the elastic together tightly twice. Cut off the extra elastic.

**time needed
3 hours**

what you need

30–35 pumpkin or melon seeds

Lilac, aquamarine and lavender blue acrylic paint

Medium paintbrush

Thick needle

30 cm (12 in) jewellery elastic

1

2

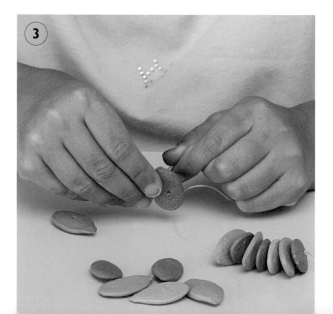

3

variations

seed necklace

Paint seeds with lavender blue acrylic paint,
leave them to dry, then dot with green paint.
Leave to dry, then repeat on the other side of
each seed. Make a hole through the top of
the seeds and thread them onto a length of
green thonging. Start with a knot, thread on
three seeds, then make another knot. Thread
on another three seeds and make a further
knot. Continue in this way until you reach
the desired length.

seed hair slide

Paint sunflower seeds with purple glitter
paint, leave to dry, then glue onto a hair slide.

tips
★ If you prefer, colour the seeds
  with waterproof felt-tipped pens.
★ Shirring elastic can be used to
  thread the seeds instead of
  jewellery elastic, if liked.

felt glasses case

ages 6–8 years

Decorate this elegant glasses case with lots of shiny sequins. The soft case is padded with a fluffy fleece lining to protect the glasses inside. It's a perfect gift for people who wear glasses, or for a friend who's going on holiday with a new pair of shades.

1 Cut two 20 x 10 cm (8 x 4 in) rectangles of turquoise felt and pink fleece for the case.

2 Thread the needle with the purple thread and sew the sequin string in a squiggle along one of the felt rectangles.

3 Thread the embroidery needle with one strand of pink embroidery thread. (An adult might need to help.) Sew the flower-shaped sequins at random along the sequin string.

4 Pin each felt rectangle onto one of the fleece rectangles. Thread the embroidery needle with three strands of pink embroidery thread. Using running stitch (see page 136), sew the layers together along the top, short edge. Remove the pins.

time needed
2 hours

what you need

Tape measure

Pencil

Scissors

23 cm (9 in) square turquoise felt

23 cm (9 in) square pink fleece

Sewing needle

Purple sewing thread

35 cm (14 in) string of purple sequins

Four flower-shaped sequins

Pink embroidery thread

Embroidery needle

Dressmaking pins

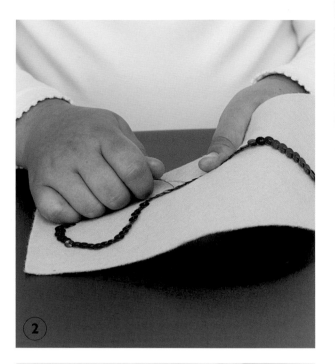

②

④

variation
spiral design

In step 2 sew spirals in running stitch using alternately embroidery thread and glittery yarn. Subsitute turquoise fleece for the padding.

tips
★ Glue the threads of the sequin string to the back of the sequins to stop them unravelling.
★ Don't use too much glue.

5 Pin both rectangles together, making sure the felt is on the outside. Using the same needle and thread, sew along the outer edges using running stitch to secure the layers together. Leave the top edge open.

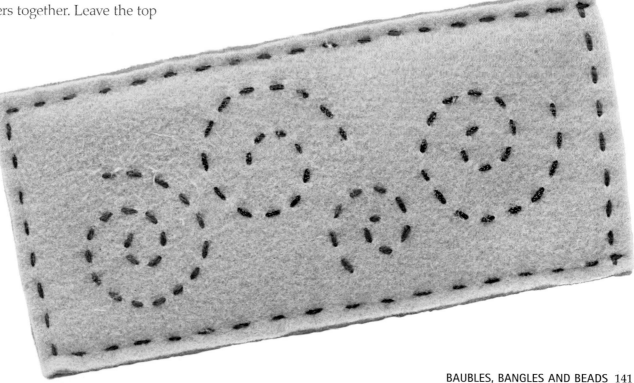

time needed
1½ hours
(excluding drying time)

what you need

Scissors

Old pair of jeans

Pink glitter paint in
easy-application
squeeze bottle

All-purpose household
glue

3 square jewellery
stones

4 heart-shaped
jewellery stones

Sewing needle

Blue sewing thread

90 cm (3 ft) each of
pink, purple and red
cord

jeans
party bag
ages 8–10 years

Recycle a pocket from an old pair of
jeans that you have grown out of to
make a fantastic party bag for a friend's
birthday. If you make two bags from
one pair of jeans, you can keep one for
yourself. Decorate the bag with glitter
paint and sparkling jewellery stones.

1 Carefully cut out one back pocket from the
jeans. (An adult may need to help if the denim is
very thick.)

2 Paint a line of pink glitter paint along the
outer edges of the pocket by squeezing it from
the bottle. The glitter paint stops the fabric
fraying. Paint along the top edge of the pocket,
then leave to dry.

3 Turn the pocket over and paint the top edge
on the wrong side of the jeans too. Leave the
pocket to dry.

4 Glue the square jewellery stones in a row
across the front of the pocket. Glue two of the
heart-shaped jewellery stones above and two
below the squares.

①

②

④

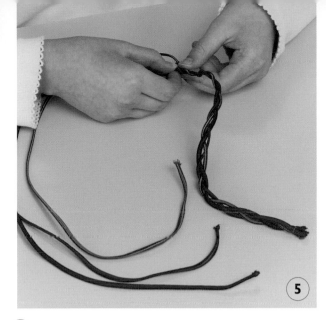

(5)

5) To make the handle, thread the needle with blue thread. Sew one end of the lengths of pink, purple and red cord together. Plait the cords, then sew the other ends together. Sew the ends of the cords inside the side edges of the pocket.

variations

flower purse

Cut a small pocket out of an old shirt (choose one with a button fastening). Paint the edges with gold glitter paint and the button with purple glitter paint. Glue a few flower-shaped sequins to the front.

fringed handbag

Cut the bottom off one leg of a pair of old colourful trousers. Glue the hem together to make a bag. Turn under the top edge and glue to make a top hem. Stick a strip of orange felt cut into a fringe across the bottom of the bag, then add a string of sequins across the top and bottom. Cut a large flower out of purple felt and a smaller flower from orange felt using the template on page 247. Glue the flowers to the bag and stick a flower-shaped sequin on top. Sew a gold braid handle inside the sides of the top of the bag.

tips
★ You might need to use adult jeans for a larger bag. Don't forget to ask permission first!
★ Rest the pocket on an old plastic carrier bag when applying glitter paint so you don't spoil your work surface.

home
sweet home

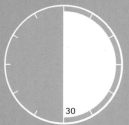

sweetheart photo frame

ages 5–6 years

Simple shapes cut out of card with added decoration of wool and beads make unusual photo frames. If you place a special photograph inside the frame this makes a very special personal gift for Father's or Mother's Day.

1 Draw a heart on the purple card using the template on page 241. Cut it out using scissors. Draw a smaller heart in the centre on the back of the card. Cut it out using the craft knife.

2 Cut a piece of pink wool and glue it to the front of the card around the cut edge of the smaller heart. Stick beads randomly onto the front of the heart.

3 Cut a square piece of blue card large enough to cover the smaller heart shape. You may need to trim the bottom corners to follow the shape of the heart. Apply glue to the sides and bottom of the blue piece and stick it down onto the back of the purple heart. The top edge should be left open to slot in the photograph.

4 To make the stand, cut out a rectangular piece of blue card and align one narrow edge with the centre of the top of the blue square. Glue it to the back of the frame so it can stand up.

**time needed
30 minutes**

what you need

Purple corrugated card
Pencil
Scissors
Craft knife
Pink wool
Coloured beads
Blue corrugated card
Glue

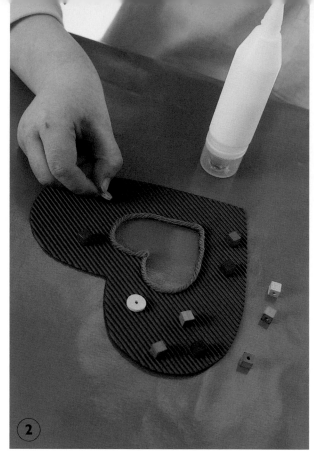

(2)

(4)

146

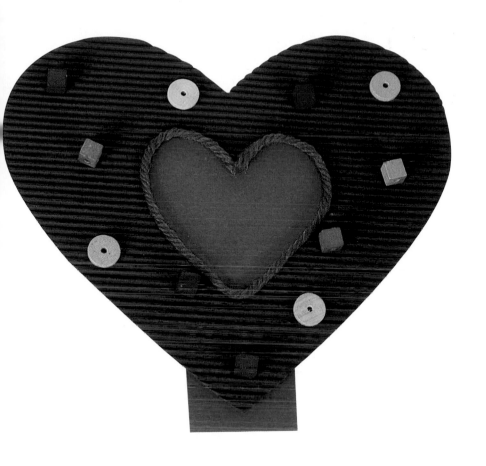

variations

square frame

This square frame is made more unusual by adding bands of contrasting strands of wool, tied and secured with a bead.

flower power

Make a flower-shaped frame in the same way and decorate with beads around the circular opening, threaded with wool knotted at the ends.

round frame

Wind wool in five different colours snugly around the frame, then decorate with wool ties and beads.

tip
★ Keep the wool even when wrapping it around the frame so it looks smooth and taut.

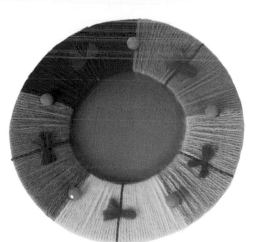

fridge magnets

ages 8–10 years

This jaunty pirate would make a super present for Father's Day. The character is made from polymer clay, which is baked until hard in the oven.

I Roll a 3 cm (1¼ in) wide ball of salmon pink clay for the face. Flatten the ball. Roll a small ball of the same coloured clay for the nose. Press the nose to the centre of the face.

2 Roll two small balls of black clay for the moustache. Pull one side of each ball upward. Press each one to the face beneath the nose.

3 Using a rolling pin, roll more black clay out to a 3 mm (⅛ in) thickness on a pastry board. Use the templates on page 249 to cut out an eye patch and tricorn hat from the clay. Position the patch on the face to one side of the nose.

4 Roll a thin sausage of black clay for the eye-patch strap and place across the face, just above the patch. Position the tricorn hat at an angle over the top of the face.

5 Slip the small metal ring to peep out from one side of the hat as an earring, then press the hat down.

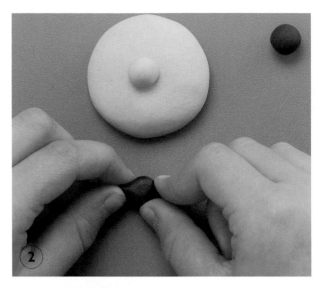

time needed
1 hour
(excluding baking and cooling time)

what you need

Salmon pink and black polymer clay

Rolling pin

Pastry board

Small metal ring (from old or broken piece of jewellery)

PVA glue

Fridge magnet

variations

teddy

Make teddy's head by flattening a
3 cm (1¼ in) ball of caramel-coloured
clay, then press on three smaller balls
for his ears and snout. Roll three even
smaller balls of black clay for the eyes
and nose. Make a bow tie from two
triangles of green clay decorated with
smaller balls of pink clay. Mark the ears
with the handle end of a paintbrush and
draw a mouth with a knife.

6 Bake the pirate in the oven following the
clay manufacturer's instructions (an adult
should help). When ready, remove from the
oven and leave to cool, then glue a fridge
magnet to the back.

strawberry

Mould a strawberry shape from a 3 cm (1¼ in)
ball of red clay. To make the leaves, flatten a
2.5 cm (1 in) ball of green clay, cut in half
and pare away V shapes in the curved edge.
Press the leaves and stalk to the top of the
strawberry. Mark seed shapes with the handle
end of a paintbrush.

flowers

Press six balls of red or purple clay around a
central ball of similar-sized yellow clay. Flatten
the 'petals' slightly and dent them with the
handle end of a paintbrush. Press six small balls
of green clay around the centre of the flower.

tip
★ Wash your hands before using a
  new colour so you don't stain
  the clay.

butterfly coaster

ages 4–5 years

Turn an ordinary opaque wall tile into a smart coaster for the table by sponging ceramic paint around a butterfly stencil. Marvel at how the butterfly emerges when you peel away the sticky-paper template. If you have time, you might like to make a set of coasters, each one a slightly different shade of green.

I Trace the butterfly template on page 249, then transfer the design onto thin card. Cut out the shape and draw around it on the sticky-backed plastic using a felt-tipped pen. (An adult may need to help with the cutting.)

2 Carefully peel off the backing paper – again, an adult might be needed to prevent it from becoming tangled – then stick the butterfly to the centre of the ceramic tile.

3 Dampen the natural sponge with a little water. Brush the green ceramic paint onto the sponge using a large paintbrush; don't put the paint on too heavily.

4 Dab the paint all over the tile, then set it aside to dry.

5 Peel off the stencil to reveal the butterfly shape beneath.

**time needed
45 minutes**
(excluding drying time)

what you need

Pencil

Tracing paper

Thin card

Scissors

Felt-tipped pen

Sticky-backed plastic

10 cm (4 in) opaque
   ceramic tile

Natural sponge

Large paintbrush

Green ceramic paint

⑤

tips
★ If you prefer a deeper colour, after allowing the first coat of paint to dry sponge on another layer of paint.
★ Make sure the sponge is not too wet before coating it with paint.
★ Wash the brush after use to prevent the bristles from hardening.

variations

oak leaf

Using the template on page 249, cut an oak leaf from sticky-backed plastic. Stick the leaf to a yellow tile, then sponge on red and white ceramic paint. Once the paint is dry, peel off the stencil.

stripes

Stick lengths of masking tape across a large tile in long stripes. Paint the gaps between the pieces of tape with ceramic paint. Leave to dry, then peel off the tape.

**time needed
2½ hours
(excluding drying time)**

what you need

Small bowl (to use as a mould)

Pastry board

Petroleum jelly (Vaseline)

Rolling pin

Air-drying clay

Knife

Drinking straw

Medium paintbrush

Wooden cocktail stick

Scissors

Kitchen towel

All-purpose household glue

Deep yellow, red and green acrylic paint

Fine red braid

cherry bowl

ages 8–10 years

This pretty bowl is decorated with clay cherries that look good enough to eat. The contrasting laced effect is made by threading fine red braid or ribbon through holes made with a drinking straw before the vessel dries.

1 Turn the small bowl upside down on the pastry board and smear the outside with the petroleum jelly (this makes it easier to slide the clay off later).

2 Using the rolling pin, roll the air-drying clay flat on the pastry board until it is about 5 mm (¼ in) thick. Lay the clay over the bowl, smoothing it over the sides. Cut the clay level around the edge with the knife.

3 Make holes around the edge of the clay using the drinking straw.

4 Roll two 2 cm (¾ in) balls of clay between your palms into cherry shapes. Make a dent across the top of each one with the paintbrush. Flatten the cherries slightly.

5 Cut a wooden cocktail stick in half with the scissors. Push each half into the top of a cherry as a stalk. Set the bowl and cherries aside to harden overnight.

6 Slide the bowl off the mould. Wipe off any remaining jelly with kitchen towel. Glue the cherries inside the bowl close to the inside edge. Leave to set.

7 Paint the bowl deep yellow and the cherries red with green stalks. Leave to dry.

8 Lace the braid through the holes around the edge of the bowl and tie the ends together.

(1)

(6)

variation

citrus bowl

At the end of step 2 cut a wavy edge around the clay bowl. Roll five 2.5 cm (1 in) balls of clay to make oranges and lemons. Squeeze the edges of two balls to form lemons. Flatten the remaining balls slightly to make oranges. When the clay has hardened, glue the fruit around the inner edge of the bowl, leave to set, then paint the bowl green and the fruit orange and yellow.

(2)

tips

★ Rest the cherries on pencil erasers or something similar inside the bowl while the glue dries.
★ Place a circle of greaseproof paper or a doily in the bowl if it's to be used for sweets that don't have wrappers.

time needed
2 hours
(excluding drying time)

what you need

Cardboard box lid
about 23 x 17 cm
(9 x 6¾ in)

Large and medium
paintbrushes

Sunshine yellow, purple
and pink acrylic paint

Pencil

Tracing paper

Masking tape

4 round stickers

PVA glue

Feather

Sharp-edged scissors

Clockwork mechanism
and hands

bird clock

ages 8–10 years

If you colour in the lid of a box using
bright paints, you can transform it into
a fabulous clock. Paint a simple bird
on the face, add the flourish of a real
feather tail and you have your very own
version of a cuckoo clock.

1 Paint the cardboard box lid with the yellow
paint and leave it to dry. Trace the clock
template on page 246 onto tracing paper.
Lightly tape the tracing paper to the box using
masking tape.

2 One by one, slip the four round stickers
beneath the tracing paper and stick them at
each quarter-hour position. Carefully remove
the tracing paper.

3 Using the template on page 246, draw a bird
beneath the clock in pencil, then paint it in
purple and pink shades.

4 When the paint has dried, glue a feather to
the back of the bird to make a tail.

5 Make a hole through the centre of the
clock with the sharp point of the scissors (an
adult might need to help). Make the hole
large enough to accommodate the clockwork
mechanism. Fix the clockwork through the hole
(follow the manufacturer's instructions), then fit
the hands to the clock.

2

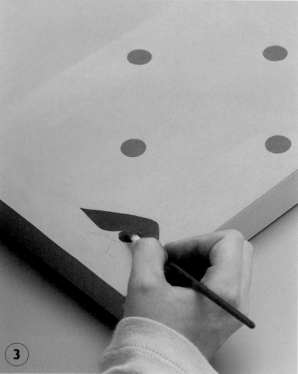

3

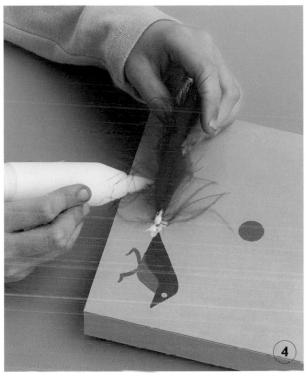

(4)

variation

bullseye clock

Paint different-coloured rings on a round cardboard box lid to resemble a target. Use the clock template as before, but this time stick silver star stickers at the quarter positions before removing the tracing paper. Finally, fit the clockwork mechanism and hands.

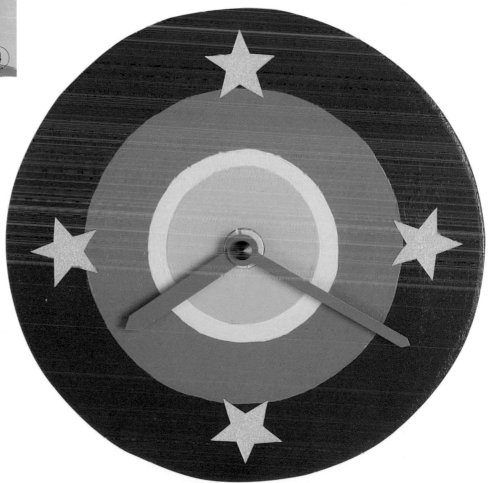

ladybird paper-weight

ages 3–5 years

This giant ladybird is not only great to look at but very useful, too, for keeping papers and letters weighted in place. The ladybird is very easy to make from air-drying clay, which hardens overnight ready for you to paint brightly next day.

1️⃣ Roll a ball of clay about 4.5 cm (1¾ in) wide between your palms. Roll the ball into an oval, then flatten it slightly. Set this ladybird shape aside to dry, which takes about a day.

2️⃣ Paint the ladybird red with a paintbrush and leave the paint to dry.

3️⃣ Paint the front of the ladybird black for its head. Paint a line along the centre of the back to divide the wings. Paint a black circle on each wing.

4 When the black paint has dried, make dots for eyes on the ladybird's head with blue paint. Leave the ladybird to dry.

**time needed
1 hour**
(excluding drying time)

what you need

Air-drying clay

Red, black and blue acrylic paint

Medium paintbrush

variations

bumble bee

Make the body of the bumble bee in the same way as the ladybird. Then roll two ovals of clay for the wings. Squeeze one side of the wings to a point. Wet the wings and the top of the bumble bee with a little water, then press the wings in place. Leave overnight to dry, then paint the body yellow. Leave to dry, then finish by painting black stripes and white wings.

tortoise

Start by making the body of the tortoise in the same way as the ladybird. Score lines on the shell with a clay modelling tool, as shown in the picture. To make the head, tail and legs, roll logs of clay then join them to the underside of the body as for the bee wings (see above). Squeeze the tail tip to a point and rest the head on a pencil while the clay dries.

time needed
1–1½ hours

what you need

Pencil

Tracing paper

Thin card

Scissors

Felt-tipped pen

23 cm (9 in) square of
fawn-coloured felt

10 cm (4 in) squares
of yellow-and red-
coloured felt

Sewing needle

Blue sewing thread

Two blue beads

Dressmaking pins

Red stranded cotton
embroidery thread

hen egg cosy

ages 8–10 years

Here is a charming hen that would make a lovely Easter present. She's very useful too, helping to keep a breakfast boiled egg nice and warm. The hen is made from coloured felt, which is easy to sew because the edges do not fray.

1 Trace the hen, beak and comb templates on page 248 then transfer the designs onto thin card. Cut out the shapes and draw around them with a felt-tipped pen as follows: a pair of hens on the fawn felt, a beak on the yellow felt and a comb on the red felt. Cut out the shapes.

2 Thread the needle with the blue thread, tying a knot in the end, then sew one blue bead on each of the hens, on the outer side where the cross is marked on the template. These will be the eyes.

3 Fold the beak in half along the broken line on the template. Pin the folded edge onto the wrong side of one hen (the side without the bead), between the dots on the side of the template.

4 Pin the comb above the beak, at the top of the hen's head, between the dots on the top of the template.

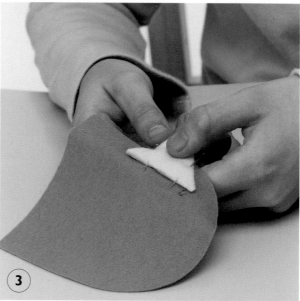

(6)

5 Pin the hens together with the wrong sides facing each other (on the inside). Make sure the beads are on the outside and in line with each other.

(6) Thread the needle with six strands of red embroidery thread (an adult might need to help to prevent tangles) and tie a knot in the end. Sew the hens together using running stitch (push the needle up from the back of the fabric to the front; pull the thread through, then push the needle from front to back a little way forward to make a straight line). Make sure you keep a 5 mm (¼ in) border between your stitches and the outside edge. (An adult might need to help.) Remove the pins.

tip
★ Make sure you sew the eyes on the opposite sides of each hen to make a matching pair of hen pieces.

variations
yellow chick
Make this cuddly chick from yellow fleece in the same way as you made the hen but leaving off the comb. Give the chick an orange beak and black bead eyes and sew it together with orange embroidery thread.

blue hen
Choose unusual colour combinations such as this blue hen with a bright pink comb and pink eyes.

time needed
2 hours
(excluding drying time)

what you need

Cardboard snack tube

Kitchen paper tube

Sweetie tube

Large and medium
 paintbrushes

Acrylic paint in shades
 of dark blue, light
 blue, turquoise,
 orange, peach and
 pink

Pair of compasses and
 pen

Thick card

Scissors

All-purpose household
 glue

desk tidy

ages 5–6 years

Brighten an untidy desk with this smart
desk tidy. Save snack, kitchen paper and
sweetie tubes to make the tidy, paint
them in brilliant colours, then fill with
pencils, pens and rulers. This makes a
perfect present for a busy office worker
or budding artist.

1 Remove the lids from the cardboard tubes
and paint the inside of each tube at the top in
one of the colours, then paint the outside the
same colour. Leave them to dry.

2 Paint wavy bands around the outside of the
tubes in contrasting colours.

3 Using the pair of compasses and pen, draw
a 14 cm (5¾ in) diameter circle on the piece of
card. (An adult might need to help.)

4 Draw a wavy edge inside the circle to create
the base. Cut out the base and paint it. Leave it
to dry.

5 Run a line of glue inside the bottom of the
kitchen paper tube and stand it on the base.
Glue first the snack tube, then the sweetie tube
to the base and to the kitchen paper tube. Let
the glue harden and dry before using.

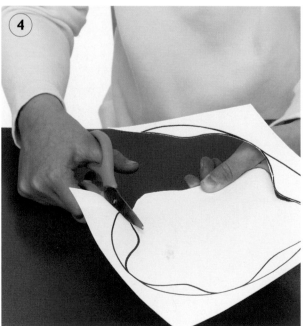

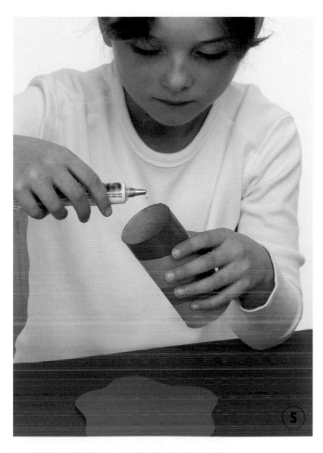

variation

money tube

Remove the lid of a cardboard snack tube.
Cut a slot in the base; this is now the top of
the money tube. Paint the tube light blue all
over and leave to dry. Paint bright blue waves
around the bottom of the tube and use a
sponge to dab white paint above the waves
as clouds. Paint a few seagulls in between.
Replace the lid on the bottom of the tube.

tips
★ Don't forget to cover the surface
  that you're working on with old
  newspaper or with a plastic
  tablecloth.
★ Decorated cardboard snack
  tubes can also make effective
  pencil cases and unusual
  treasure boxes.

striped cat napkin ring

ages 5–6 years

Amuse guests with a set of cute striped cat napkin rings at a celebration meal. They can take their cats home with them to remind them of the wonderful time they've had. If you make one for each guest, you could even write names on the cat's tummy so everyone knows where to sit.

1   Cut out one section from the egg box. Glue a cotton pulp ball on top for the head.

(2) Trace the cat ear template on page 249 then transfer the design twice onto thin card. Cut out the ears, fold them in half and glue them to the top of the head.

(3) Paint the cat pale orange. Leave to dry.

(4) Glue the red pompom to the head as a nose. Draw eyes with the black felt-tipped pen.

(5) Draw furry patterns over the cat with the orange felt-tipped pen. Make a hole at the back of the body and glue the orange pipecleaner inside it for the tail. When you lay the table, wind the tail around a napkin.

**time needed
1½ hours**

what you need

Cardboard egg box

All-purpose household glue

3 cm (1½ in) cotton pulp ball

Pencil

Tracing paper

Thin card

Scissors

Medium paintbrush

Pale orange acrylic paint

5 mm (¼ in) red pompom

Black and orange felt-tipped pens

Orange pipecleaner

162

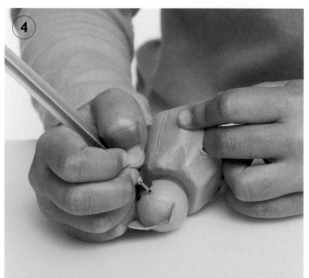

variations

bird

In step 2, use the template on page 249 to cut a beak, fold it in half and glue to the front of the head. Paint the beak yellow and the bird blue. Leave to dry, then stick on two joggle eyes. Glue feathers and chenille pipecleaners to the back of the bird, winding one pipecleaner around a napkin.

snowman

Paint the body and head white. Cut a strip of felt, using zig-zag scissors along one long edge. Glue around the head. Stick a pompom to the head as a nose. Draw eyes with black pen. Glue a button to the front of the snowman. Wrap a pipecleaner around the neck as a scarf, winding the end around a napkin.

elephant

In step 2, use the template on page 249 to cut two ears from pink card, then glue to the sides of the head. Paint the elephant pale pink. Make a hole in the front of the head. Glue a pale pink pipecleaner into the hole for a trunk. Draw eyes with a black pen. Wind the trunk around a napkin.

tip
★ Cotton pulp balls are cheap to buy from craft shops.

time needed
20 minutes

what you need

Coloured tissue paper

Pencil

Scissors

Glitter glue

Glass

Stick glue

Candle

candle-holders

ages 4–6 years

Make these beautiful candleholders for family or friends for a special festival or enjoy them at home anytime. The coloured tissue paper gives a glowing vibrant colour, it's easy to apply and fun for children to decorate with sparkle, sequins and beads.

1 Choose the glass you are going to use and cut a piece of green tissue paper large enough to fit around it. Apply stick glue lightly to the paper and wrap it around glass. Press it against the surface so it sticks. Don't worry if the paper creases as this gives more interest when a candle is lit inside the glass. Trim any excess tissue paper from the top of the glass.

2 Cut small strips of turquoise tissue paper. Make the same number of cerise-coloured stars and dot them with glitter glue. Stick the stars to the tops of the turquoise strips.

3 Glue the non-star end of the turquoise strips along the inside rim of the glass then fold them over the edge so that the stars are hanging down. Put a candle in the glass.

variations

- Try using tissue paper in clashing colours. Make decorative trims around the rim of the glass using sequins and torn paper. Decorate the sides of the glass as well.

- A blue tissue paper-covered glass embellished with silver sequin-braid and large flowers has extra sparkle.

tips
- ★ Recycle glass jars and containers instead of buying glasses.
- ★ Night-lights are safer to use than ordinary household candles.
- ★ Remember that water-based glues will dissolve tissue paper.

CAUTION!
Be very careful with lighted candles. Always ask an adult to light the candles and never leave them unattended.

fishy bookmark

ages 5–6 years

A wavy bookmark decorated with a foam fish is a great gift for a keen reader, and looks sweet as it pokes out from the top of the pages. Add more sparkle by sticking on silver sequins to look like bubbles. If you have lots of foam and fancy a more adventurous project, try making the pretty purse shown in the variations opposite.

**time needed
45 minutes**

what you need

Pencil

Tracing paper

Thin card

Scissors

Black felt-tipped pen

Aquamarine, blue and bright pink neoprene foam

All-purpose household glue

5 silver sequins

1 Trace the bookmark template on page 251 then transfer the design onto thin card. Cut out the shape and draw around it on the aquamarine foam with the black felt-tipped pen. Similarly, cut a fish from the blue foam. Draw an eye on the fish with the black felt-tipped pen.

2 Using the template on page 251, cut scales and tail details from the bright pink foam and a fin from aquamarine foam.

3 Glue the scales and tail details, then the fin, onto the fish. Glue the fish to the top of the bookmark.

4 As a finishing touch, glue silver sequins to the bookmark as bubbles. Leave the bookmark to dry before using.

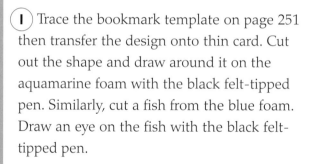

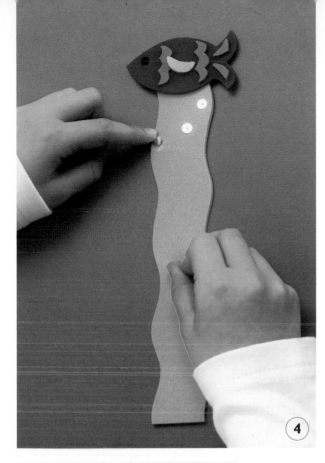

④

variations

shell bookmark
Cut a 20 x 3.5 cm (8 x 1⅜ in) strip of yellow foam. Use the template on page 251 to cut a shell from red foam. Glue the shell to the yellow strip. Paint green lines on the shell and spots on the bookmark.

pink purse
Cut out a purse shape from pink foam using the template on page 251. Fold the front up along the broken lines on the template and sew at the sides with plastic thonging (an adult might need to help to keep it neat). Fasten the flap at the front by sticking on a hook and loop fastening spot (available from craft shops). As a finishing touch, cut a starfish from aquamarine foam using the template on page 251, glue onto the flap and dot with bright pink paint.

pebble
pets

ages 5–6 years

Make this sweet-looking panda for a favourite friend, who's sure to treasure it. All you have to do is paint a nice, round pebble to make the pet, then glue on some funny joggle eyes.

1 Paint the pebble white all over using the large paintbrush. Leave to dry.

2 Paint a black band around the middle of the pebble to make the body.

3 Still using the black paint but with the medium paintbrush, paint patches for the nose and eyes, then the ears. Leave to dry.

4 Glue the joggle eyes onto the eye patches. Set aside until the glue is dry. Draw in a smile with the pink felt-tipped pen.

45

**time needed
45 minutes**
(excluding drying time)

what you need

Large pebble

White and black acrylic paint

Large and medium paintbrushes

All-purpose household glue

2 joggle eyes

Pink felt-tipped pen

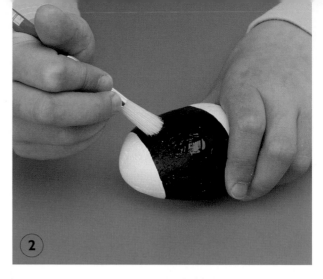

variations

lion

Choose a large pebble, paint it pale orange and leave to dry. Draw on nose, mouth, eyes and whisker dots with a black waterproof pen. Then paint the mane in stripes of yellow and bright orange paint. Plait lengths of orange wool and make a knot at the end. Glue the plait beneath the lion for a tail.

mouse

Paint a tiny pebble light pink and leave to dry. Dot on eyes with a black waterproof pen. Paint the ears in a deeper pink using a smaller paintbrush. Stick on a tiny red pompom for the nose. Finally, glue a length of plastic thong beneath the mouse for a tail.

rabbit

Paint a pebble grey and leave to dry. Paint on rabbit ears using pink paint and a smaller brush. Draw a nose and mouth using pink and black waterproof pens. Glue joggle eyes above the nose and stick on a white pompom tail.

tip
★ Large painted pebbles make ideal paper-weights.

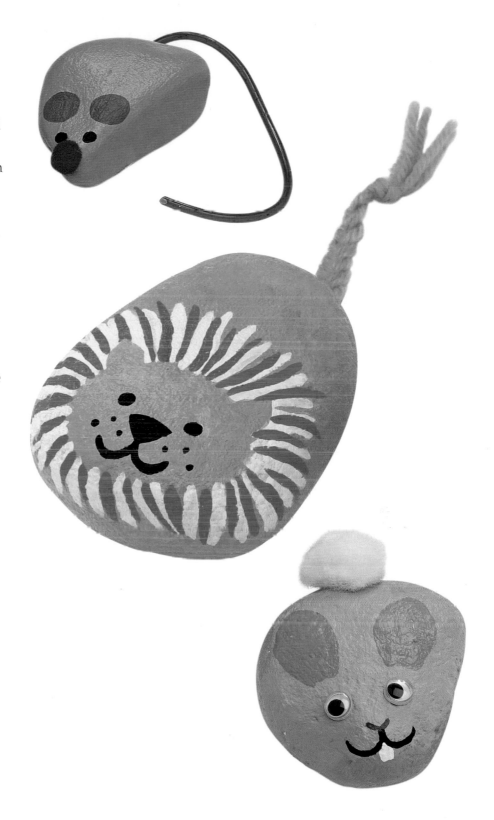

painted plant pot

ages 3-4 years

Here is an excellent gift for garden lovers – a plant pot painted in lively colours then stamped with a bold flower design. Choose the colours for the pot to suit the gardener's own preferences. You can buy ready-made flower stamps from craft and stationery shops. Present your gift filled with a favourite plant or a pot of herbs.

time needed 1½ hours (excluding drying time)

what you need

- Square terracotta plant pot
- Lavender blue, yellow and orange acrylic paint
- Large and fine paintbrushes
- Large flower rubber stamp

1 Paint the plant pot lavender blue on the outside using the large paintbrush. Using the same colour, paint inside the pot at the top. Leave to dry.

2 Use the medium paintbrush to apply yellow paint to the flower motif on the rubber stamp. Don't put on too much paint or the outline of the flower will come out smudged.

3 Stamp the flower carefully but firmly onto each side of the plant pot. Set aside to dry.

4 Dot orange paint onto the centre of the flower and allow to dry before using the pot.

variations

yellow spattered pot

Paint a terracotta pot yellow all over, including on the inner edge. Leave to dry. Cover your work table and surrounding area with plenty of old newspaper and put on an apron or old shirt, then use an old toothbrush to spatter paint in contrasting colours all over the outside of the pot. Leave to dry. Wash your hands well after spattering.

pink sponged pot

This time, paint a terracotta plant pot pale pink all over, then leave to dry. Dab deep pink paint over the outside of the pot using a sponge. Leave to dry, then paint the rim of the pot aquamarine.

tip
★ You can make your own stamp by cutting a shape from neoprene foam. Glue it to a piece of thick card then paint the foam ready for stamping.

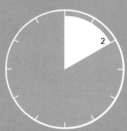

time needed
2 hours

bird feeder

ages 8–10 years

Hang a birdfeeder in a garden and just watch the birds flock in. This makes a perfect present for a nature lover. Why not wrap up a bird-spotting book with it so the recipient can enjoy recognizing the different species?

1 Measure the circumference of one plastic lid. Use a pair of metal cutters to cut a rectangle of wire mesh 18 cm (7¼ in) high and 2 cm (¾ in) longer than the circumference of the lid.

2 Using the needle, make a row of holes around the edge of one of the plastic lids; this will be the base. (An adult might need to help younger children with this task.)

③ Bend the mesh into a cylinder, overlapping the ends. Stand the cylinder upright inside the base. Starting at the overlap, oversew the bottom of the mesh to the base by sewing through the holes in the mesh then the holes in the base with fine wire, pulling the wire tight after each hole. When you have worked all the way around, twist the ends of the wire together.

④ Oversew the overlapped edges of the mesh together.

what you need

Ruler

2 plastic lids of the same size

Metal cutters

Wire mesh

Thick needle

Fine wire

Purple wire

8 assorted purple and pink beads

Small pair of pliers

Packet of peanuts

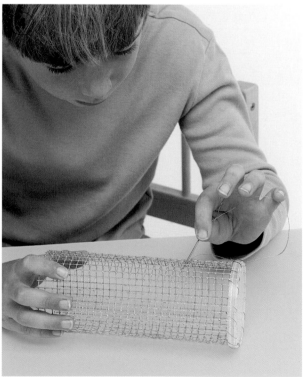

variation

nightlight holder

Thread beads onto coloured wire, then wrap the wire tightly around the rim of a preserve jar. Twist the ends of the wire securely together. Make a beaded handle, as before, and hook the ends onto the wire on either side of the jar. Place a nightlight inside.

CAUTION!

Be very careful with lit candles. For safety, always ask an adult to light the candle and never leave a lit candle burning unattended.

5 Snip a 25 cm (10 in) length of purple wire to make a handle. Bend one end into a loop with the pliers. Thread four beads onto each end of the handle. Make a loop at the other end of the handle. Hook the looped ends onto each side of the top of the wire feeder.

6 Pour in the peanuts and place the other lid on top of the feeder.

tip
★ Hang the feeder high up where cats and other animals cannot reach it.

pressed-flower box

ages 8–10 years

Collecting and pressing flowers and leaves is a great hobby, especially if you use them to make gifts like this sweet box. It would be a lovely present to give on Mother's Day, filled with yummy edible treats (see pages 200–235).

1   Paint the outside of the box and lid with lilac paint. Leave to dry, then paint the inside of the box red.

2   Hold a pressed yellow flower with a pair of tweezers. Spread a little glue over the back of the flower with the cocktail stick, then stick the flower on the centre of the lid.

3   Glue three red pressed flowers around the edge of the lid, then stick three white flowers between them, using the tweezers and cocktail stick as before.

4   Glue single red and purple petals around the rim of the lid using the tweezers and cocktail stick as before. Leave to dry.

5   Put the lid on the box. Glue pairs of leaves around the side of the box using the tweezers and cocktail stick as before.

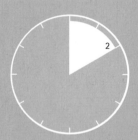

**time needed
2 hours**
(excluding drying time)

what you need

Small box with lid

Lilac and red acrylic paint

Large paintbrush

Assorted pressed flowers and leaves

Pair of tweezers

PVA glue

Cocktail stick

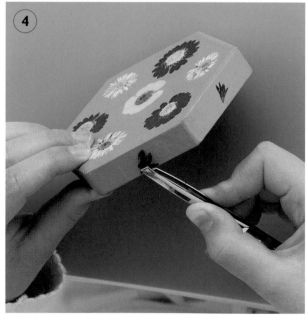

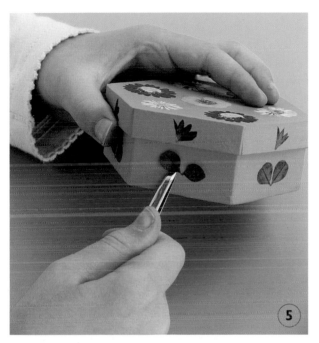

variations

pressed-flower picture

Tear strips of coloured, textured paper and stick them to a piece of white paper. Glue pressed flowers and flower-shaped stickers in rows to the torn strips of paper. Place the picture in a frame. Decorate the frame with flower-shaped stickers.

mirror frame

Glue pressed rose buds on stems to the frame surrounding a mirror. Leave to dry on a flat surface before hanging on the wall.

tips
★ To press flowers, place picked garden flower heads on one side of a piece of blotting paper. Fold the blotting paper over the top of the flowers. Press the flowers between the pages of a heavy book or in a flower press. Carefully remove the flowers after a few weeks.
★ Coat the box and its lid with PVA glue once you have placed all the flowers to seal them in place.

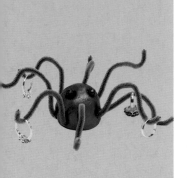

octopus ring holder

ages 3–4 years

Luckily, this amusing octopus has enough legs to hold lots of jewellery. He is made from air-drying clay and his bendy legs are pipecleaners. An older sister might like him as a present.

**time needed
1 hour**
(excluding drying time)

what you need

Air-drying clay

2 beads

4 lilac pipecleaners

Aquamarine and pearlized green acrylic paint

Large paintbrush

All-purpose household glue

1 Roll a 5 cm (2 in) wide ball of clay between your palms to make the octopus body. Rest the octopus on your work surface. Press the beads into the top of the octopus to dent the clay at the top, where his eyes should be. Remove the beads.

2 Cut the pipecleaners into eight 12 cm (4¾ in) lengths for the legs. Push the legs into the octopus toward the bottom of his body, four on each side, then remove them. Set the octopus aside to harden.

3 Paint the octopus with the aquamarine paint. Leave to dry, then paint over the top with the pearlized paint.

4 Glue the eyes to the head in the eye holes. Dab glue on the end of each leg and poke them into the holes you made. (An adult might need to help.) Bend the legs in a curve. Set aside until the glue is dry.

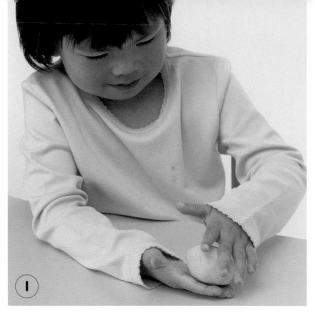

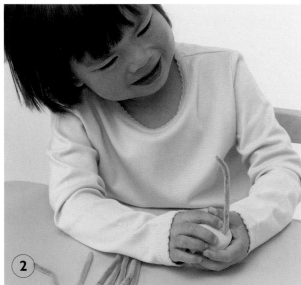

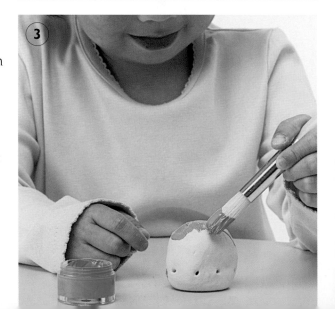

④

tips

★ The insects can also be used for hanging earrings on.

★ Make sure you cover the work surface before you get out the clay and paint.

★ You can recycle coloured plastic packaging to make insect wings.

variations

striped insect

Roll a 5 cm (2 in) wide ball of clay into an oval shape for this exotic insect. Press two beads into one end to dent the clay. Remove the beads. Cut white pipecleaners into six 12 cm (4¾ in) lengths for the legs. Push three legs into each side of the insect, then remove them. Leave the clay to harden, then paint the insect in stripes. Glue the bead eyes and pipecleaner legs in place.

blue insect

Make the insect body as above, pressing in and taking out the beads and legs. Using the template on page 249, cut two wings from green plastic, then make two slits on the top of the body using the wings. Remove the wings. Leave the clay to harden overnight. Paint the insect with blue pearlized paint. Glue the bead eyes and yellow chenille pipecleaner legs in place, bending them up. Glue the wings into the slits.

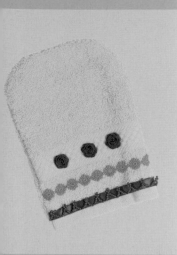

**time needed
1½ hours**

what you need

Tape measure

Pencil

Scissors

2 face flannels

Dressmaking pins

16 cm (6½ in) bead
    edging

Matching sewing
    threads

Sewing needle

15 cm (6 in) flower lace

Three ribbon roses

bath mitt

ages 6–8 years

Here is a luxurious present for someone who deserves to be pampered. It's a bath mitt made from two face flannels and trimmed with colourful beads, lace and ribbon roses. If you are giving this to your mum as a gift, make sure you also give her an hour's peace once a week for maximum enjoyment.

1 Cut a 21 x 16 cm (8½ x 6½ in) rectangle from one of the face flannels, making sure one of the short edges runs along one of the flannel's hemmed edges. Cut the opposite short edge in a curve.

2 In exactly the same way, cut another mitt to match from the second flannel.

3 Pin the bead edging along the bottom of one mitt. Thread up the needle with matching thread, then sew the edging in place using running stitch (see page 159). (An adult might need to help at this stage.) Remove the pins.

4 Pin and sew the flower lace across the mitt above the bead edging. Remove the pins.

5 Sew the ribbon roses in a neat row above the flower lace.

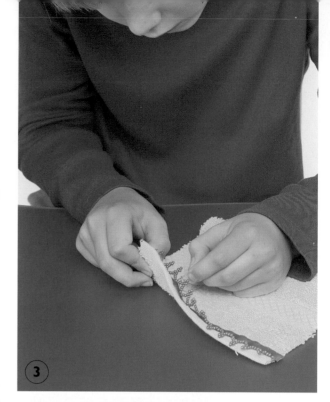

variation

ric-rac mitt

Make the mitt as before but this time using dark blue flannels. Sew rows of ric-rac and flower lace across the centre of one side of the mitt.

6 Pin the mitts together with the right sides facing each other (on the inside). Sew along both sides and the top leaving the bottom edge open. Remove the pins and turn the mitt to the right side.

tips
★ Make the mitt in colours to match the bathroom of the person you are giving it to.
★ Dab glue on the ends of the bead edging to stop the beads falling off.

smells nice

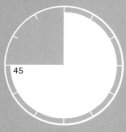

what you need

Pencil

Tracing paper

Thin card

Scissors

1 sheet natural beeswax

1 sheet red beeswax

9 cm (3¾ in) candle wick

beeswax candle

ages 6–8 years

Roll an elegant candle from two coloured strips of beeswax, then enjoy the honey-sweet scent as it burns. Sheets of beeswax are available from craft shops or specialist candle-making suppliers and websites.

1 Trace the candle template on page 250 twice, once along the narrow line and once along the wide line, then transfer the shapes onto thin card. Cut out the shapes and draw around the wide strip on the natural beeswax and the narrow strip on the red beeswax with a pencil. Cut out both strips. Lay the narrow red strip over the wide natural strip with the lower, long edges level.

2 From the leftover natural beeswax, cut a piece about 2 x 2 cm (¾ x ¾ in). Roll it around one end of the wick.

3 Turn over the two beeswax strips and lay the wick along the longest side edge of the layered beeswax strips and start to roll the strips around the wick.

4 Once you have finished rolling the candle, press the short ends of beeswax smoothly to the candle to prevent it from unravelling.

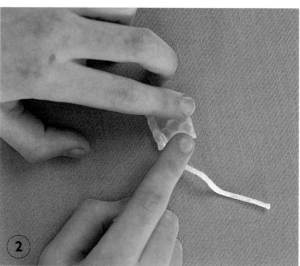
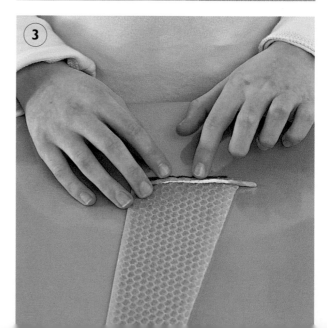

(4)

variations

triple spiral candle

Roll three layers of beeswax in contrasting colours. Cut one wide strip of beeswax and one narrow strip as before, then cut a medium-width strip, each one in a different colour. Stack the strips with the bottom edges level, as before, then roll carefully around the wick.

straight beeswax candle

Coil two straight strips of red beeswax together around a wick. Cut the ends level and press them to the candle.

appliqué candle

Appliqué wax, available from craft shops, is a thin layer of wax that can be cut out and stuck to candles. Cut a zig-zag strip of gold appliqué wax and a few triangles from gold and blue appliqué wax. Press the pieces in a pattern around a pink candle.

tip

★ Sheets of beeswax are best handled with warm hands and the beeswax is easier to roll if it is not cold. Warm the sheets with a hair drier if the room is cold.

CAUTION!

Be very careful with lit candles. For safety, always ask an adult to light the candle and never leave a lit candle burning unattended.

**time needed
45 minutes**

what you need

Approx. 200 g (7 oz)
Epsom salts

Clear container with lid

Bowl

Vanilla essence

Tablespoon

Red and yellow
cosmetic colourings

All-purpose household
glue

Artificial flower

bath salts

ages 6–7 years

It is very simple to make coloured bath salts for Mum or Granny by adding a tiny amount of cosmetic colouring to Epsom salts. Pour the salts into a clear container so the colour shows through and glue a flamboyant artificial flower to the lid as an attractive finishing touch. Even better, make your own flower decoration by following the instructions on pages 50–51.

1 Pour the Epsom salts into the final container to measure exactly the amount you need. Then tip them into a bowl.

2 Add one drop of vanilla essence to scent the salts. Stir the mixture with a tablespoon.

3 Add 2 drops each of the red and yellow cosmetic colourings. Be careful not to add more than this amount. Stir in the colouring until all the salts turn pale orange.

4 Spoon the mixture into the container. Screw the lid on tightly. Glue the artificial flower to the lid.

(3)

(4)

tips

★ Be extra careful not to colour your clothing and the floor!

★ Add less colour than you think you need – a few drops go a very long way. It's easy to add more colour if you need to, but impossible to take colour away.

★ Epsom salts are available from pharmacies and natural health stores.

★ Cosmetic colourings are available from craft stores and soap-making websites.

variation

two-tone bath salts

Colour the salts with a few drops of blue cosmetic colour to give a pale blue. Divide the salts in half, placing them in two bowls. Colour one half with a few more drops of blue cosmetic colour to give a deeper blue. Holding the container at an angle, pour the dark blue salts into your container, then pour the pale blue salts on top, filling to the top. Screw on the lid. Glue an artificial flower on the lid, as before.

CAUTION!

Be careful not to get the Epsom salts on your skin, and wash your hands well with soap and water after finishing the project. Open a window to keep the room well ventilated while you work.

Epsom salts are not recommended for use by pregnant women, young children or people who have high blood pressure or heart disease.

lavender pillow

ages 8–10 years

Sweet-smelling lavender is known to help us sleep, so what better filling could there be for a pretty hand-painted pillow? Give it to a friend to keep on her bed, or to a tired parent who complains about lack of sleep.

1 Cut two 28 x 20 cm (11½ x 8 in) rectangles from the pink cotton fabric for the pillow-case. Trace the lavender sprigs template on page 246 and transfer it into the middle of one rectangle.

2 Paint over the stems of the lavender sprigs with the light green fabric paint, tracing over the pencil lines.

3 Paint the flowers with the pale pink paint using the fine paintbrush. Leave the paint to dry, then iron the wrong side of the fabric to fix the paint, following the manufacturer's instructions.

4 Cut the scallop-shaped lace in half. Pin each piece to the painted rectangle 5 cm (2 in) in from the two short edges. Thread up the needle with the cream-coloured thread, knot the end, and sew the lace in place using running stitch (see page 159). (An adult might need to help.) Remove the pins.

time needed
2 hours

what you need

Ruler

Pencil

Scissors

20 cm (8 in) of 90 cm (36 in) wide lightweight pink cotton fabric

Tracing paper

Fine paintbrush

Light green and pale pink fabric paint

40 cm (16 in) scallop-shaped lace

Dressmaking pins

Cream and pink thread

Sewing needle

Toy filling

Handful of dried lavender

3

4

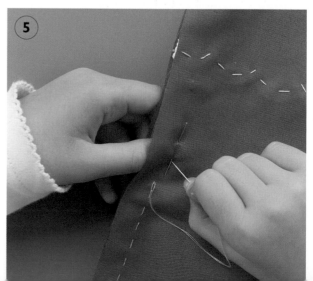

5

variation
rose pillow

Cut the pillow from lightweight lilac cotton fabric. Sew purple and gold ribbon diagonally across two corners of one rectangle. Following the template on page 246, paint a cream rose bud on the pillow. Fix the paint by ironing, as before, and make up the cushion when the paint has dried, pouring in a handful of fragrant dried rose buds (these can also aid sleep). Apply a touch of gold glitter paint to the flower.

5 Pin the rectangles together with the right sides facing (painted side inside). Thread up the needle with the pink thread, knot the end and sew along the outer edges to stitch the layers together, using running stitch. Leave an opening on the lower edge. Remove the pins

6 Turn the pillow inside out through the opening in the lower edge so the painted side is on the outside. Fill the pillow with the toy filling by stuffing it through the opening on the lower edge. Pour a handful of lavender into the front of the pillow. Sew the opening closed.

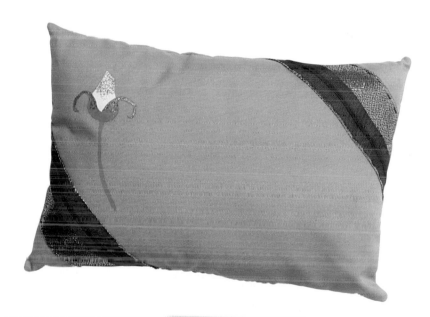

tips
★ After sewing, carefully cut across the seam allowance on the corners; this helps the fabric to lie neatly when you turn it to the right side.
★ Try not to make the stitches too long or the lavender may slip between them and escape from the pillow.

novelty soaps

ages 8–10 years

No one will believe these pretty heart soaps are homemade. If you can't source a heart-shaped flexible ice tray at a local hardware or homeware store, choose one in the shape of stars or even penguins!

1 Place the soap in the top of the double boiler or into the bowl on top of the saucepan filled with a little hot water. (An adult should be at hand to supervise). Heat the boiler or bring the water in the pan to the boil and watch as the soap melts. Turn off the heat.

2 Put on the gloves and add a few drops of the red cosmetic colour, stirring it in with the wooden spoon.

3 Carefully pour the melted soap into the moulds of the flexible ice tray (an adult should do this).

4 Leave the soaps to harden for about two hours, then turn them out of the ice tray.

5 Nestle the soaps in a small basket lined with crumpled cellophane.

**time needed
45 minutes**
(excluding hardening time)

what you need

200 g (7 oz) glycerine soap

Double boiler or heatproof bowl and saucepan (the bowl should sit snugly on top)

Thin protective gloves

Red cosmetic colouring

Wooden spoon

Flexible heart-shaped ice tray or other novelty shape

Small basket

Sheet of cellophane

(4)

variation
string of star soaps

Make deep blue and light blue star-shaped soaps in a
flexible star-shaped ice tray. When the surface has hardened
(but the soaps aren't hard all the way through), make a hole
through the centre of each star. Leave the soaps to harden
completely, then thread a double length of narrow ribbon
through the holes, leaving a loop at the top and making a
knot between each star.

tips
★ Cosmetic colouring is available from craft shops and soap-
  making websites, but if you can't find it easily, substitute a
  few drops of food colouring to colour the soaps.
★ When working with cosmetic dyes, wash your hands well
  with soap and water after finishing the project.

**time needed
45 minutes**

what you need

White doily

Scissors

Sprigs of rosemary, thyme, dill and parsley

Elastic band

Orange raffia

tussie mussie

ages 4–6 years

In ancient times, posies of sweet-smelling herbs called tussie mussies were often carried to hide nasty smells. But they are attractive in their own right, too. This tussie mussie is framed by a delicate paper doily and it makes a beautifully scented bouquet that would be a lovely gift to give to mum on Mother's Day morning.

1 Fold the doily lightly into quarters, pinching the folds at the centre. Cut a small hole at the centre with the scissors.

2 Bunch together the sprigs of rosemary and thyme. Add the sprigs of dill and parsley around the outside to make a pretty posy.

3 Fasten the elastic band around the stems to secure them, making sure the herbs are held tightly together.

4 Slip the stalks carefully down through the hole in the doily so that the lacy part of the doily frames the greenery nicely.

5 Bunch together a few lengths of raffia and tie them in a bow around the tussie mussie beneath the doily.

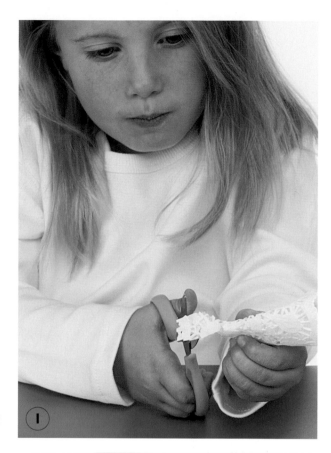

1

2

tip
★ If you are not presenting the tussie mussie immediately, dampen some kitchen paper and wrap it around the stems then wrap securely in clingfilm.

variation

bouquet garni

Keen cooks will welcome this gift to add flavour to their cooking. Bunch together a few stalks of parsley, a sprig of thyme and a bay leaf, then tie together at the stalks with string ready to throw into a casserole or soup.

lip balm

ages 6–8 years

A luscious pot of vanilla-scented lip balm will be much appreciated by mum, an auntie or another favourite grown-up for keeping lips smooth and glossy. Decorate the tiny container with a shiny sticker and curly ribbon to make it even more special for Mother's Day or for a birthday.

(1) Put on the gloves and spoon the petroleum jelly and a little of the lipstick (if using) into the bowl. Add 2–3 drops of the vanilla essence.

(2) Mix the ingredients together by mashing them with the back of the spoon until they are blended smoothly.

(3) Spoon the balm into the small pot. Screw the lid on tight and wipe away any sticky mess from the pot or lid using a clean kitchen towel or sponge.

(4) Stick the heart-shaped sticker on the top of the pot's lid. Tie gift-wrapping ribbon around the outside of the lid. Starting at the knot, pull each end of the ribbon along the blade of a blunt knife to curl it. (An adult might need to help.) If it doesn't curl the first time, try again, keeping the ribbon taut on the blade of the knife all the way along.

**time needed
1 hour**

what you need

Thin protective gloves

2 dessert spoons of petroleum jelly (Vaseline)

New lipstick (optional)

Mixing bowl

Vanilla essence

Spoon

Small pot with lid

Clean kitchen towel or sponge

Heart-shaped sticker

Silver curling gift wrapping ribbon

Blunt knife

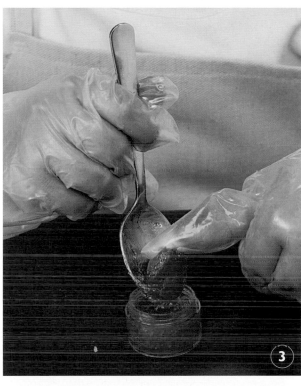

tip
★ Thin protective gloves are
needed when making the lip
balm as it's quite a messy job.

variation

glitter pots

Mini preserve jars make excellent containers for
lip balm. After washing the pots and lids well
(preferably in a dishwasher, leaving them inside
until cool and dry), decorate them with stickers
and glitter paint.

CAUTION!

Don't use old lipstick for this –
it might contain germs.

sugar scrub

ages 4–6 years

This fragrant skin scrub for a mum or aunt leaves skin silky smooth and glowing and is the perfect gift for someone special who deserves a little pampering at bathtime. It's especially good for sloughing off rough skin on elbows and heels. Make sure you give this gift to a grown-up only.

1) Mix together the sugar and olive oil in the bowl to make a gloopy mixture. Stir in the almond essence.

2) Carefully spoon the mixture into the air-tight pot and screw on the lid. Wipe away any spilt mixture on the pot with a clean cloth.

3 Write a special message on the gift tag. Thread the gift tag onto a length of the gift-wrapping ribbon.

4) Ask an adult to pull the blunt blade of the knife along each end of the ribbon to curl it. Finally, tie the ribbon with a knot around the lid of the pot.

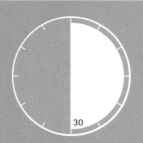

**time needed
30 minutes**

what you need

70 g (2¾ oz) granulated sugar

2 dessert spoons olive oil

Mixing bowl

½ teaspoon almond essence

Small air-tight pot with lid

Clean cloth

Pen

Gift tag

Gift-wrapping ribbon

Blunt knife

(4)

variation
fragrant bath bag

Place a tablespoon of fine oatmeal and a handful each of dried thyme and lavender in the centre of an 18 cm (7¼ in) circle of muslin cut with zig-zag scissors. Gather up the outer edges of the circle and tie them with a length of ribbon. As the water runs through the muslin, it carries the lovely fragrance into the water, while the oatmeal makes the water silky soft. Only give this gift to an adult, and do not give to pregnant women.

tip
★ Tell the recipient to rub the sugar scrub gently over damp skin, then rinse off with plenty of warm water. Do not use on the face. You could write these instructions on the gift tag in your best writing.

christingle candles

ages 3–6 years

Christingle oranges have a wonderfully spicy aroma. Cloves are relatively easy for little fingers to push into an orange, just make sure to protect the surfaces from the juice! It's easy to make lots of interesting patterns and the oranges look especially attractive with candles in them either for use at home or for the Christingle service at church.

1 Cut several cocktail sticks in half and push each one through a cranberry. Decorate your orange with a line of cranberries, pushing one in at a time.

2 Add two lines of cloves to the orange, above and below the cranberries.

3 Use an apple corer to scoop out the centre of the orange and place a candle in the hole (this is best done by an adult).

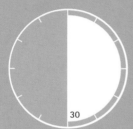

time needed
30 minutes

what you need

Cocktail sticks

Scissors

Cranberries

Orange

Cloves

Apple corer

Candle

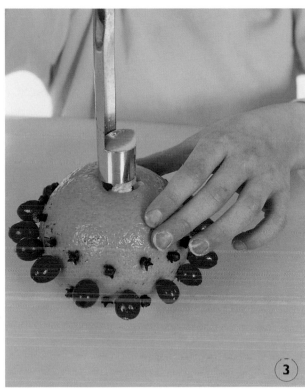

variations

Try making different patterns on your Christingle orange with circles or lines of cloves, or wrap a ribbon around it.

tips

★ Make your Christingle orange just before it is needed as they look better freshly made.
★ Try using them as a table decoration or centrepiece with sprigs of holly or fir.

fragrant sachet

ages 6–8 years

This fragrant drawer sachet keeps clothes smelling sweet. It is made from scraps of fabric and netting and you only need a handful of pot pourri or lavender to fill it. Cut out the heart shapes using zig-zag scissors to stop the edge of the fabrics from fraying. A heart-shaped button makes a delightful finishing touch.

1 Trace the heart template on page 250 then transfer the design onto thin card. Cut out the heart and draw around it with a black felt-tipped pen on the pink fabric and netting. Cut out both hearts with the zig-zag scissors.

2 Use a cotton bud to run a line of glue around the outer edge of the pink fabric heart, leaving the top edge free from glue. Press the net heart on top. Hold in place while drying.

3 Pour the pot pourri or lavender into the sachet through the hole in the top of the heart.

4 Run another line of glue around the top of the heart. Press the netting onto it firmly to close the sachet and prevent its contents from escaping. Finally, glue the heart-shaped button to the front of the sachet. Set aside to dry.

**time needed
45 minutes**

what you need

Pencil

Tracing paper

Thin card

Scissors

Black felt-tipped pen

Zig-zag scissors

Pink fabric

Pink netting

Cotton bud

PVA glue

Handful of pot pourri or dried lavender

Heart-shaped button

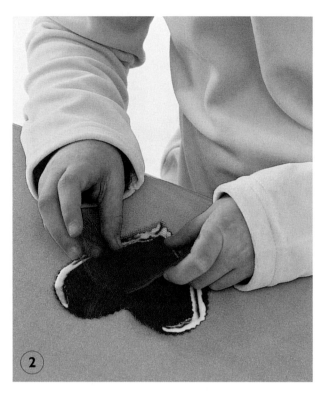

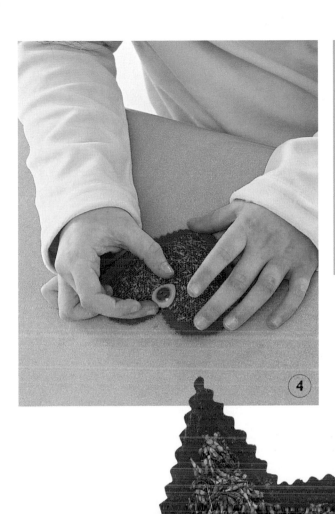

tips
★ Fill the sachet over a sheet of paper, then you can tip any spilt lavender or pot pourri mix back into its container.
★ Don't worry if you can't find a button that's heart-shaped; just go for one in a colour that matches.
★ Refresh pot pourri with 1–2 drops of essential oil of lavender every few months if the scent fades. (Have an adult on hand to prevent too many drops of essential oil from spilling out.)

4

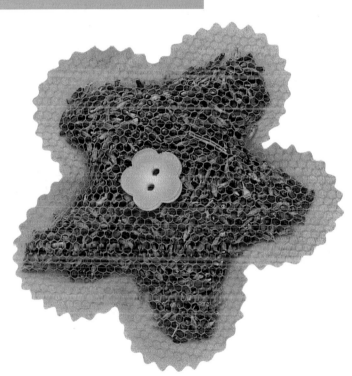

variation
stars and flowers sachets
Cut out the fabric and netting in the shape of a star or flower, using the templates on page 250, then finish with a button matching the colour or shape of the sachet.

yummy for your tummy

halloween lanterns

ages 8–10 years

These lanterns are made out of oranges instead of pumpkins. Get everyone to have a go at creating scary faces for a delicious halloween party treat.

1 On the chopping board, cut a slice off the top of each orange, about one-third down from the top, and put to one side. Using the teaspoon, scoop out the orange flesh and membrane until you reach the white inside of the orange.

2 Turn one of the oranges on its side and carefully cut eye and mouth shapes with the small sharp knife – get adult help if necessary. You may prefer to mark these on with a pen before you begin cutting. Do the same with the other oranges.

3 Fill with scoops of ice cream, sorbet or jelly. Replace the lids, place sliced cherries into the mouths and add strips of unwound liquorice for hair. Serve immediately or put in the freezer until ready to serve.

**time needed
45 minutes**

what you need

4 oranges

4 scoops vanilla ice cream or blackcurrant sorbet or set jelly

4 liquorice Catherine wheels

Few glacé cherries

Chopping board

Small serrated knife

Teaspoon

Ice cream scoop

tip

★ Other fruits, such as a grapefruit, small watermelons or yellow-skinned melons, could also be used as lanterns.
★ Use the unused orange flesh to add to a fruit salad. Alternatively, to make a smoothie, blend the orange flesh with a banana and some yogurt in a liquidizer.

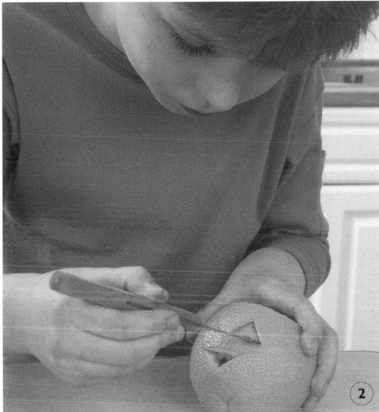

stained glass windows

ages 6–8 years

These cookies are great fun to make. Broken boiled sweets are placed in the middle of biscuits with a hole in them and when they are baked the sweets melt to form colourful windows.

**time needed
45 minutes**
(plus cooking and cooling)

what you need

125 g (4 oz) butter

175 g (6 oz) plain flour

50 g (2 oz) caster sugar

½ small orange, rind only

Few clear coloured boiled sweets

2 baking sheets

Nonstick baking paper

Knife

Chopping board or plate

Mixing bowl

Electric mixer (optional)

Grater

Rolling pin

Selection of large and small biscuit cutters

Ovengloves

1 Set the oven to 180°C/350°F/ Gas Mark 4. Line the baking sheets with the nonstick baking paper. Cut the butter into small squares, then put into the mixing bowl with the flour and sugar. Rub in the butter using your fingertips or an electric mixer until the mixture looks like fine crumbs. Grate the orange rind finely, then stir it into bowl.

2 Squeeze the mixture together with your hands to make a ball. Roll out thinly on a surface dusted with flour. Stamp out large window shapes using the biscuit cutters. Put on to the paper-lined sheets, then stamp out smaller shapes from the centre of each biscuit and remove.

3 Re-knead the biscuit trimmings, roll out and continue cutting biscuits until all the mixture is used. Bake in the oven for 8–10 minutes until pale golden.

4 Meanwhile, unwrap the sweets and break with the rolling pin. Carefully remove the sheet of biscuits from the oven. Add different coloured pieces to the hole in each biscuit – get adult help with this because the biscuits will be hot. Bake in the oven for a further 2–3 minutes until the sweets have just melted. Leave to cool, then peel the biscuits off the paper and serve.

tip

★ Similar biscuits can be made to hang on the Christmas tree, but use a firmer biscuit mixture, such as the one on page 206. Make tiny holes in the top of each biscuit with the end of a teaspoon as soon as they come out of the oven.

chocolate tree decorations

ages 6–8 years

These chocolate tree biscuits will look lovely when they are hung on your Christmas tree. Decorate them all in the same style or let everyone in family do something different.

**time needed
45 minutes**
(plus cooking and cooling)

what you need

75 g (3 oz) butter

3 tablespoons golden syrup

150 g (5 oz) caster sugar

325 g (11 oz) plain flour

15 g (½ oz) cocoa

1 teaspoon ground cinnamon

2 teaspoons bicarbonate of soda

4 tablespoons milk

1 tube ready-to-use white writing icing

Mini candy-coated chocolate drops or other tiny sweets

Fine ribbon, to finish

2 baking sheets

Pastry brush

Saucepan

Wooden spoon

Sieve

Bowl

Rolling pin

Large Christmas tree cutters or other festive cookie cutters

Teaspoon

Palette knife

1 Set the oven to 180°C/350°F/ Gas Mark 4. Brush the baking sheets with oil using the pastry brush. Put the butter, syrup and sugar in the saucepan. Heat gently, stirring with a wooden spoon, until the butter has melted.

2 Sift the flour, cocoa, cinnamon and bicarbonate of soda into the bowl, then add to the melted butter mixture with the milk. Mix to a smooth ball. Leave for 5 minutes or until cool enough to handle.

3 Knead until evenly coloured, then roll out on a lightly floured surface until it is 5 mm (¼ inch) thick. Stamp out Christmas shapes with the cutters, then transfer to the baking sheets. Re-roll the trimmings and continue cutting shapes until all the dough is used.

4 Bake in the oven for 10–12 minutes until just beginning to darken. Make a hole in the top of each biscuit with the end of a teaspoon, then leave to cool on the sheets.

5 Pipe on white icing to decorate by squeezing the icing straight from the tube. Decorate with sweets and leave to harden. Thread fine ribbon through the hole at the top of each biscuit, then tie on to the Christmas tree. Eat within 3 days.

tip

★ If the dough gets too stiff to re-roll the trimmings, warm the dough in the microwave on Full Power for 20 30 seconds, depending on the amount of dough.

candy canes

ages 4–8 years

Make these stripy candy canes as a gift for a birthday or for Mother's or Father's Day. Everyone will want to eat these deliciously minty sweets.

**time needed
30 minutes**
(plus overnight to harden)

what you need

1 sachet dried egg white (or the equivalent of 2 egg whites)

Few drops peppermint essence

550 g (1 lb 2 oz) icing sugar

Little red liquid or paste food colouring

Mixing bowl or food processor

Fork

Sieve

Wooden spoon

Plastic gloves (optional)

Trays

Nonstick baking paper

Boxes lined with waxed or greaseproof paper

1 Put the dried egg white into the bowl or bowl of the food processor. Mix in the water – check with the packet instructions for the quantity. Add the peppermint essence, then gradually sift in the icing sugar, a little at a time, mixing with the wooden spoon to make a smooth paste. As the mixture gets stiffer, squeeze together with your hands.

2 Add some red food colouring to the mixture and knead, stopping when the colours are only half-mixed together and still look swirly. Use plastic gloves, if liked.

3 Shape and roll pieces of icing into thin ropes on a work surface dusted with extra icing sugar until about 1 cm (½ inch) thick. Cut to 12 cm (5 inch) lengths. Curl the tops to resemble walking canes. Dry overnight on trays lined with nonstick baking paper.

4 Pack the canes into small boxes lined with waxed or greaseproof paper. Use within 1 week.

tip

★ For very young children, keep the mixture to just one colour, then roll out and stamp shapes using small biscuit cutters.

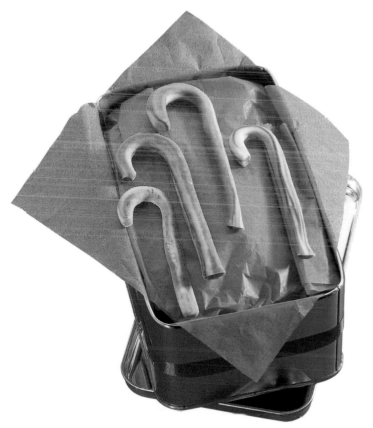

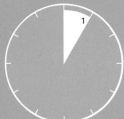

**time needed
1 hour**
(plus hardening)

what you need

50 g (2 oz) dark chocolate

250 g (8 oz) white marzipan or ready-to-roll decoration icing

Red, yellow and green paste food colourings

1 medium plain chocolate Easter egg

Sifted icing sugar, for dusting

Cellophane and ribbon, for wrapping

Small bowl

Saucepan or microwave

Small knife

Chopping board

Small rolling pin

Small sieve

Easter egg faces

ages 6–10 years

Turn a simple Easter egg into something special by decorating it with coloured marzipan. Use your imagination to create a whole family of Easter egg faces or why not make Easter animals instead?

1 Break the chocolate into pieces and melt in the bowl set over a saucepan of just boiled water. Alternatively, melt the chocolate in the microwave for 1½ minutes on Full Power or according to manufacturer's instructions.

2 Divide the marzipan or decoration icing into four pieces. Keep one piece white and colour the rest, using red, yellow and green food colourings.

3 Unwrap the chocolate egg.

4 Roll out or mould small pieces of coloured marzipan or icing at a time into eyes, mouth, hair, ears, nose, feet and whatever features you would like your face to have. (Dust your hands and the work surface with a little sifted icing sugar if the marzipan or icing begins to stick.) Stick the facial features on to the eggs using dots of melted chocolate.

5 Allow the decorated egg to harden. Wrap each egg in Cellophane and tie with ribbon.

Easter chocolate nests

ages 4–8 years

Who could resist these little chicks sitting on top of a chocolate nest. Make sure you bake enough because they'll disappear fast!

1 Set the oven to 180°C/350°F/ Gas Mark 4. Place the paper cases into the sections of the muffin tin.

2 Put the cocoa powder, margarine or butter, sugar, flour, cocoa and eggs into the bowl. Beat together with the wooden spoon or electric mixer until smooth.

3 Spoon the mixture into the paper cases so that they are half-filled. Bake in the centre of the oven for 12–15 minutes until well risen and the tops spring back when pressed lightly with a finger. Leave to cool.

4 Take the cakes out of the tin and spread the tops with the chocolate spread, using the butter knife. Break the crumbly chocolate bar into pieces and arrange on top of the cakes to look like nests. Add the mini eggs and chicks, if using.

**time needed
30 minutes**
(plus cooking and cooling)

what you need

15 g (½ oz) cocoa powder

125 g (4 oz) soft margarine or butter, at room temperature

125 g (4 oz) caster sugar

100 g (3½ oz) self-raising flour

2 eggs

4 tablespoons chocolate spread

3 crumbly chocolate bars

200 g (7 oz) mini eggs

Few Easter chick decorations (optional)

12 paper cake or medium muffin cases

12-hole cake or muffin tin

Fine sieve

Mixing bowl

Wooden spoon or electric mixer

Dessertspoon

Oven gloves

Butter knife

iced cookies

ages 6–10 years

These tasty biscuits are not just easy to make, they are fun to decorate with ready-made coloured icing. Bake them for a birthday party and let guests customize one each, or stamp them out using Christmas- or Easter-shaped cutters for seasonal celebrations.

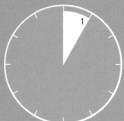

**time needed
1 hour**
(plus resting and baking)

what you need

75 g (3 oz) butter

75 g (3 oz) granulated sugar

1 rounded tablespoon golden syrup

Mixing bowl

Wooden spoon

1 egg

Sieve

375 g (12 oz) self-raising flour, plus extra for dusting

½ teaspoon ground cinnamon

1 teaspoon ground ginger

Pastry board

Rolling pin

Star-shaped cookie cutter

Nonstick baking paper

Baking sheet

Wire rack

2 tablespoons apricot jam

Small saucepan

Pastry brush

1 pack ready-to-roll red icing

Coloured sugar pearls

Gift box

Tissue paper

1 Place the butter, sugar and golden syrup in the mixing bowl and cream together with the wooden spoon. Now beat in the egg.

2 Sieve the flour, cinnamon and ginger into the creamed mixture. Stir the mixture, then knead it to a firm dough. Set the dough aside for 40 minutes to rest.

3 Lightly dust the pastry board with flour. Roll the dough out flat, about 5 mm (¼ in) thick. Stamp out lots of star shapes with the star-shaped cutter. Place them on a sheet of nonstick baking paper on a baking sheet.

4 Place the baking sheet in a preheated oven, 160°C (325°F), Gas Mark 3, for 15 minutes. (An adult should assist at this stage.) Remove from the oven and allow to cool on the wire rack.

5 Warm the apricot jam in the small pan and brush onto the centre of a star.

6 Roll a ball of red icing 2 cm (¾ in) in diameter. Flatten the ball between your fingers and press onto the centre of the star. Press coloured sugar pearls into the icing to make circles or other patterns.

7 When the icing has set, place the biscuits in the gift box.

variation
daisy biscuits

Cut out the biscuits using a daisy-shaped cutter. When decorating them, place a circle of green icing at the centre of each biscuit, then press an icing flower in the middle, and decorate with coloured pearl 'petals'.

tip
★ Cover a small box with gift wrap that suits the personality of the person you are giving the biscuits to before arranging them inside.
★ These iced cookies will keep in a sealed container for one week.

white chocolate truffles

ages 6–10 years

Delicious vanilla-flavoured white chocolate truffles are a favourite with any chocolate lover. When you make them yourself, you don't have to save them up as a special treat; give them as a little present when a friend needs cheering up.

**time needed
1 hour**
(plus cooling)

what you need

150 g (5 oz) white chocolate

80 g (3¼ oz) unsalted butter

Double boiler, or heatproof bowl and saucepan (the bowl on top)

Wooden spoon

½ teaspoon vanilla essence

2 egg yolks, lightly beaten

Mixing bowl

Whisk

Pastry board

Clingfilm

Dessert spoon

40 g (1½ oz) icing sugar

Plate

Nonstick baking paper

Scissors

Coloured tissue paper

Gift box

1 Roughly break up the chocolate. Cut the butter into small pieces. Slowly melt the chocolate and butter pieces in the double boiler or in the bowl on top of the saucepan filled with a little hot water. (An adult should be at hand to supervise.) Stir with the wooden spoon.

2 Remove from the heat and stir in the vanilla essence.

3 Tip the egg yolks into a mixing bowl. Gradually whisk the warm chocolate mixture into the eggs. Cover the bowl with clingfilm and place in the refrigerator for about 8 hours, to firm.

4 Place the chocolate mixture on a pastry board. Scoop up some of the mixture with the dessert spoon and roll between your palms into a ball. Repeat until you have used up the chocolate mixture.

5 Sprinkle the icing sugar over the plate. Then roll the balls in the sugar and set on a sheet of baking paper.

6 Cut pieces of coloured tissue paper and baking paper just large enough to line the gift box. Cut the edges in a zig-zag shape. Place first the tissue paper, then the baking paper in the box. Fill the box with the truffles.

variation

milk chocolate truffles

Instead of using white chocolate, substitute milk chocolate. Then, in step 5, roll the balls in grated chocolate rather than icing sugar.

tips

★ Make sure you have cool hands when you roll the chocolate mixture into balls to prevent it from melting as you work. Run your hands under a cold tap and dry well if you find them warming up.

★ These truffles will keep for 5 days in a sealed container in the refrigerator. You could write this instruction on the bottom of the gift box with a pretty-coloured pen or on a label in your best handwriting.

gingerbread decorations

ages 2–6 years

Gingerbread cookies are very festive for this time of the year. If you can possibly resist eating them, hang them on the Christmas tree or wrap them up to give as a gift.

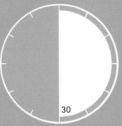

**time needed
30 minutes**
(plus cooking and cooling)

what you need

For the gingerbread:

75 g (3 oz) butter

3 tablespoons golden syrup

150 g (5 oz) light muscovado sugar

375 g (12 oz) plain flour

2 teaspoons bicarbonate of soda

1 teaspoon ground ginger

1 teaspoon ground cinnamon

1 egg, beaten

1–3 tablespoons milk

Rolling pin

Pastry board

Gingerbread cutter (or cardboard template)

To decorate:

275 g (9 oz) icing sugar, sieved

4 tablespoons warm water

Red writing icing

Silver balls

Thin red ribbon

1 Preheat the oven to 180°C/ 350°F/Gas Mark 4. Melt the butter, syrup and sugar in a saucepan, stirring until smooth. Mix together the flour, bicarbonate of soda and spices and stir into the pan, adding the beaten egg and enough milk to make a smooth dough.

2 When the dough is cool enough to handle, knead and roll it out on a lightly floured surface to a thickness of 5 mm (¼ in). Cut out as many biscuits as you can with the gingerbread cutter (or use a small knife to cut around a cardboard template). Transfer to a greased baking sheet.

3 Bake the gingerbread cookies for 8–10 minutes in the preheated oven until the dough begins to darken. Remove from the oven and leave to cool.

4 Mix the icing sugar with the warm water. Decorate the surface with white icing and silver balls then draw on the detail with red writing icing. Allow the icing to dry and tie a narrow ribbon around the neck.

(2)

(4)

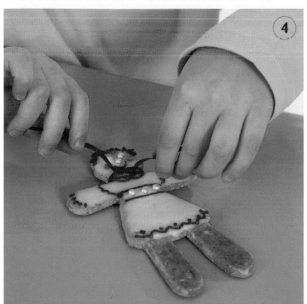

(4)

variations
all shapes and sizes

Using different shaped cutters will give great variety to your assortment of biscuits especially when they are decorated with coloured icing, iced stars and multi-coloured dots.

tip
★ Always pierce a hole in a biscuit before you bake it if you want to thread a ribbon through. Make it a good size as they can close up during cooking.

time needed
30 minutes
(plus overnight to harden)

what you need

175 g (6 oz) butter, softened

Mixing bowl

1 small can sweetened condensed milk –approximately 175 g (6 oz)

800 g (1¾ lb) icing sugar, sieved

Pastry board

Rolling pin

Wire rack

Tea towel

Chocolate buttons

Sweet cases

Star box or tissue paper nest

no-cook fudge

ages 4–6 years

These no-cook fudge goodies gift-wrapped in a pretty, shaped box make a quick stylish present – just don't eat too many or you won't have enough to give away.

1 Put the softened butter into a bowl and stir in the condensed milk. Gradually add the sieved icing sugar.

2 When it is mixed together, turn the fudge onto a pastry board and knead until it is smooth and easy to handle.

3 Roll out the fudge with a rolling pin to a thickness of 1 cm (½ in) and cut it into strips and then into neat squares.

4 Put a chocolate drop onto some of the squares if you wish. Leave overnight on a wire rack covered with a tea towel to harden.

5 Place the squares in sweet cases and pop in a box or make a nest of tissue paper.

variations

other flavours

Experiment with different flavours by adding a few drops of vanilla or peppermint essence to the fudge mixture. Or sieve 75 g (3 oz) of cocoa with the icing sugar to make chocolate fudge.

chocolate hearts

Use a small heart cutter and make lots of fudge hearts or make a giant one that can be wrapped individually in cellophane.

tips
★ If the mixture is too thin, add more sieved icing sugar.
★ Roll the fudge out smoothly otherwise the surface will look cracked.
★ Use a dab of icing to stick the chocolate buttons (or other cake decorations) to the fudge squares.

coconut ice

ages 6–8 years

To make this yummy gift look extra special, display the pastel colours of the coconut ice to best advantage by presenting them in an attractive glass jar tied with matching or contrasting coloured ribbon.

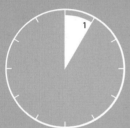

time needed
1 hour

what you need

500 g (1 lb) granulated sugar

150 ml (¼ pint) milk

Saucepan

Wooden spoon

150 g (5 oz) desiccated coconut

2 drops vanilla essence

20 cm (8 in) square baking tin or pie dish, oiled

Pink food colouring

Blunt knife

Air-tight glass jar

1 Place the sugar and milk in the pan and heat, stirring with the wooden spoon, so that the sugar dissolves. Bring the mixture to the boil and continue cooking for ten minutes. (An adult should supervise at this stage.)

2 Remove the pan from the heat and let the bubbles subside. Stir in the desiccated coconut with the spoon. Add the drops of vanilla essence.

3 Spoon half of the coconut mixture into the baking tin or pie dish, pressing gently with the back of the spoon to even out the surface, if necessary.

4 Stir a few drops of pink food colouring into the remaining mixture to give it a delicate pink colour. Spoon this mixture carefully over the first half of the mixture in the tin and flatten gently with the back of the spoon, if required.

5 Before it is completely cold, cut the coconut ice into pieces using the blunt knife.

6 When the coconut ice is cold, carefully remove the squares and place in the air-tight glass container and secure the lid.

variation
icy blue coconut ice

In step 4, instead of tinting the ice pink, substitute a few drops of blue food colouring. Once the coconut ice is completely cold, put the coconut ice in a cardboard cone filled with contrasting-coloured shredded tissue paper.

tip
★ Use a cookie cutter to stamp the coconut ice into simple shapes, such as hearts, stars, circles or diamonds.

peppermint creams

ages 4–6 years

Make these heart-shaped confections as a romantic gift for Valentine's Day. (Mums and dads will love them.) Make sure you disguise your identity as the sender of the gift to add an extra element of surprise on the big day.

(1) Sieve the icing sugar into the bowl. Add the beaten egg white and the water.

(2) Stir the mixture to a smooth paste with the spoon, then add the peppermint essence. Be careful not to add more than 2 drops. Set the mixture aside for 10 minutes.

3 Lightly dust a sheet of baking foil with icing sugar. Roll the paste out flat, about 1 cm (½ in) thick.

(4) Stamp out heart shapes with the cookie cutter, rerolling the mixture as necessary. Set them aside to dry overnight.

5 Fill the gift box with shredded tissue paper, then place the peppermint creams on top.

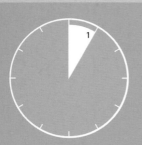

**time needed
1 hour**
(plus drying)

what you need

Sieve

500 g (1 lb) icing sugar, plus extra for dusting

Mixing bowl

1 egg white, beaten

1 tablespoon water

Wooden spoon

2 drops peppermint essence

Baking foil

Rolling pin

Heart-shaped cookie cutter

Gift box

Shredded tissue paper

(1)

variation
disc-shaped creams

Instead of cutting out heart shapes, roll small balls of peppermint-cream mixture and flatten them into disc shapes. Set aside to dry as before, then place in a box.

224

tip
★ Gently roll a pastry wheel across the surface of the peppermint creams to make a wavy pattern on the top.

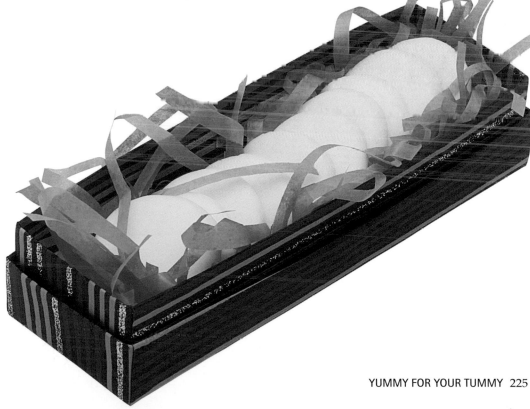

noah's ark cookies

ages 4–6 years

Decorating these delightful animal cookies will keep children happy on a rainy day.

**time needed
30 minutes**
(plus cooking and cooling)

what you need

175 g (6 oz) butter, at room temperature

75 g (3 oz) caster sugar

275 g (9 oz) plain flour

To finish

tubes of different coloured writing icing

mini candy-coated chocolate sweets

kitchen scales

round-bladed knife

plate

large mixing bowl

electric mixer (optional)

nonstick baking paper

rolling pin

animal-shaped cookie cutters

palette knife

baking sheets

wire rack

1 Set the oven to 180°C/350°F/ Gas Mark 4. Cut the butter into small pieces on the plate then put in the bowl with the sugar and flour. Rub the butter into the flour mixture between your fingertips to make tiny crumbs, or use an electric mixer. Using your hands squeeze the cookie crumbs together to make a dough. Knead lightly then cut in half.

2 Place one of the pieces of cookie dough between 2 large sheets of nonstick baking paper then roll out thinly. Peel off the top piece of paper and stamp out animal shapes using a selection of different cookie cutters, making 2 of each animal shape.

3 Carefully lift the cookie animals with the palette knife and place on the ungreased baking sheets. Add the cookie trimmings to the other half of the cookie dough and squeeze together back into a ball. Continue rolling and stamping out the mixture until it has all been shaped into animals.

4 Bake the cookies for about 10 minutes until they are pale golden. Leave to cool on the baking sheets, or transfer to the wire rack if preferred.

5 When the cookies are cold, let your imagination run riot as you add the animal markings, piping features with tubes of coloured icing and adding sweets for eyes. Set the cookies aside for 30 minutes for the icing to harden before serving. They can be stored in an airtight tin for up to 2 days.

(2)

(5)

(2)

tips
★ Rolling out cookie mixture can be tricky for small children, so rolling it between 2 sheets of nonstick baking paper helps to stop it sticking and breaking apart.
★ For chocolate-flavoured animals, use 15 g (½ oz) less flour, adding cocoa powder in its place.

shortbread spirals

ages 4–6 years

These wonderful shortbread spirals are really easy to make. All you have to do is roll the two different doughs together, cut into slices and bake.

**time needed
30 minutes**
(plus cooking and cooling)

what you need

2 tablespoons cocoa powder

1 tablespoon boiling water

200 g (7 oz) butter, at room temperature

300 g (10 oz) plain flour

100 g (3½ oz) caster sugar

1 teaspoon vanilla essence

Kitchen scales and measuring spoons

Small mug

Teaspoon

Round-bladed knife

Plate

2 mixing bowls

Electric mixer (optional)

Rolling pin

Nonstick baking paper

Large baking sheet

1 Set the oven to 160°C/325°F/ Gas Mark 3. Put the cocoa powder into the mug and mix with the boiling water until smooth.

2 Cut the butter into small pieces on the plate then put it in a mixing bowl with the flour and sugar. Rub the butter into the flour mixture with your fingertips to make tiny crumbs, or use an electric mixer.

3 Spoon half the cookie mixture into the second bowl, add the cocoa paste to one and the vanilla essence to the other. Squeeze the crumbs and cocoa paste together with your hands until the crumbs begin to stick together and form an evenly coloured dough. Wash your hands and repeat with the remaining crumbs and the vanilla essence.

4 Roll out the cocoa dough between 2 sheets of nonstick baking paper to make a 20 cm (8 inch) square. Do the same with the vanilla dough, using another 2 sheets of nonstick baking paper. Peel the top sheets off each piece of dough. Put the cocoa dough on top of the vanilla dough so that the base paper you were rolling out on is now on top. Peel this off then roll up the double cookie mixture into a long roll, peeling away the other sheet of paper as you go. Chill for 15 minutes.

5 Cut the roll into 16 thick slices. Place on an ungreased baking sheet and cook for 8–10 minutes. Leave the cookies to cool on the baking sheet before serving.

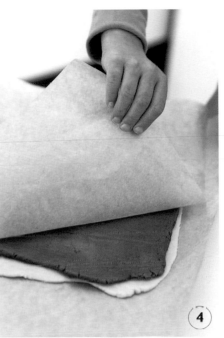

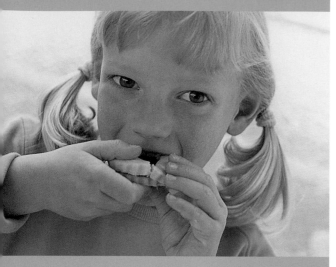

sweetheart cookies

ages 4–6 years

Treat friends and family to a very pretty treat on Valentine's Day with these sweetheart cookies. Either serve them at a party or wrap them up to give as a gift.

**time needed
30 minutes**
(plus cooking and cooling)

what you need

oil, for greasing

200 g (7 oz) plain flour, plus a little extra for dusting the work surface

25 g (1 oz) custard powder

50 g (2 oz) caster sugar

150 g (5 oz) butter, at room temperature

1 egg yolk

4 tablespoons seedless raspberry jam

Sifted icing sugar, to decorate

Pastry brush

2 baking sheets

Kitchen scales and measuring spoons

Large mixing bowl

Round-bladed knife

Plate

Electric mixer (optional)

Rolling pin

6 cm (2½ inch) fluted round cookie cutter

3 cm (1¼ inch) heart-shaped cookie cutter

Small sharp knife

Palette knife

Small sieve

1 Set the oven to 160°C/325°F/ Gas Mark 3. Lightly brush the baking sheets with a little oil.

2 Put the flour, custard powder and sugar in the bowl. Cut the butter into pieces on the plate then add to the bowl. Rub the butter into the flour mixture between your fingertips to make tiny crumbs, or use an electric mixer.

3 Stir in the egg yolk and mix to a smooth dough, first with the round-bladed knife then with your hands when the dough becomes too stiff to stir.

4 Knead the dough on a surface sprinkled with a little flour then cut it in half and roll out one half until about 5 mm (¼ inch) thick. Stamp out large circles using the round cookie cutter. Cut out little hearts from the centre of half the circles, using the heart-shaped cutter, and lift out with the end of the small sharp knife. Transfer the rounds to the oiled baking sheets. Squeeze the trimmings together and roll out with the remaining dough, stamping out shapes until you have 15 circles with heart-shaped centres cut out and 15 whole circles.

5 Bake the cookies for 10–12
minutes – slightly less for the
heart-stamped ones – until they
are pale golden. Loosen the
cookies with the palette knife and
leave to cool on the baking sheets.
They can be stored in an airtight
tin for up to 2 days.

6 To serve, spread the jam over
the whole cookies, top with the
heart-stamped ones then dust
with a little sifted icing sugar.

bat biscuits

age 4–6 years

Biscuits are always popular and these bat-shaped ones are no exception. They are great for a party and make wonderfully appropriate trick or treats. Get everyone to have a go at creating a template of some creepy creature or shape.

1 Melt the butter, syrup and sugar in a saucepan, stirring until smooth. Mix the flour, bicarbonate of soda and spices in a mixing bowl, then stir them into the pan, adding the beaten egg and enough milk to make a smooth dough.

2 Preheat the oven to 180°C/350°F/Gas Mark 4. When the dough is cool enough to handle, knead and roll it out on a lightly floured surface to a thickness of 5 mm (¼ in). Cut out as many biscuits as you can with a bat-shaped cutter (or cut around your own card template with a small knife). Transfer to a greased baking sheet.

3 Make holes in the top of each biscuit with a skewer. Bake for 8–10 minutes in the preheated oven until the dough begins to darken. Remake the holes in the biscuits while they are still soft and leave to cool.

4 Meanwhile make the icing. Mix the icing sugar with a little black food colouring then gradually add warm water. Once the biscuits are cool, use a knife to cover each biscuit with icing. Before the icing dries, sprinkle each bat with edible bronze glitter.

**time needed
45 minutes**
(plus cooking and cooling)

what you need

For the biscuits:

75 g (3 oz) butter

3 tablespoons golden syrup

150 g (5 oz) light muscovado sugar

Saucepan

375 g (12 oz) plain flour, sieved

2 teaspoons bicarbonate of soda

1 teaspoon ground ginger

1 teaspoon ground cinnamon

Mixing bowl

1 egg, beaten

1–3 tablespoons milk

Pastry board

Rolling pin

Bat-shaped biscuit cutter (or card template and knife)

Baking sheet

To decorate:

275 g (9 oz) icing sugar, sieved

4 tablespoons warm water

Black food colouring

Edible bronze glitter

variations

Make a selection of different shaped biscuits and decorate them with orange, black and white icing, glitter shapes and liquorice strips. Make your own creepy templates to use instead of biscuit cutters.

tip
★ Edible glitter colours come in small pots, but a little goes a long way. A small pinch is sufficient to cover one of these iced biscuits.

sparkling cakes

ages 4–6 years

A selection of decorated fairy cakes is always a treat for friends and family alike. Edible glitter looks wonderful and makes rather ordinary looking cakes and biscuits into something special and exciting. These cakes are perfect for a carnival party. Beware of the glitter: it goes everywhere and can stay on hands and face for hours!

**time needed
30 minutes**
(plus cooking and cooling)

what you need

Cake mixture:

125 g (4 oz) soft margarine

125 g (4 oz) caster sugar

125 g (4 oz) self-raising flour, sifted

2 eggs

Mixing bowl (or electric mixer)

Wooden spoon

Plain paper cake cases

12-hole bun tin

Wire rack

To decorate:

Bowl

Spoon

225 g (8 oz) icing sugar, sieved

2–3 tablespoons water

Blue edible glitter

Foil parasol

Glitter glue, sequins for paper cases

Bowl and spoon

1 Preheat the oven to 180°C/350°F/Gas Mark 4. Place all the cake ingredients in a mixing bowl and blend with a wooden spoon. You can use an electic mixer if you prefer.

2 Spoon the mixture evenly into 12 paper cake cases. Bake in the preheated oven for 15–18 minutes. Remove and leave to cool on a wire rack.

3 Meanwhile, make the icing by mixing the icing sugar with the water. When the cakes are cool, spread the tops with icing.

4 Sprinkle each cake generously with edible blue glitter.

5 Decorate the paper cases with glitter glue and finish with a foil parasol.

tips

★ Sprinkle the edible glitter onto the icing before it has set.
★ Buy decorated cases if you don't want to make your own.

variations

glittering patterns
Sprinkle the glitter in lines, dots and criss-cross for different effects.

decorated cases
Sequins, glitter glue and pre-gummed shapes make a plain paper case look eye-catching – no one will be able to resist them.

templates

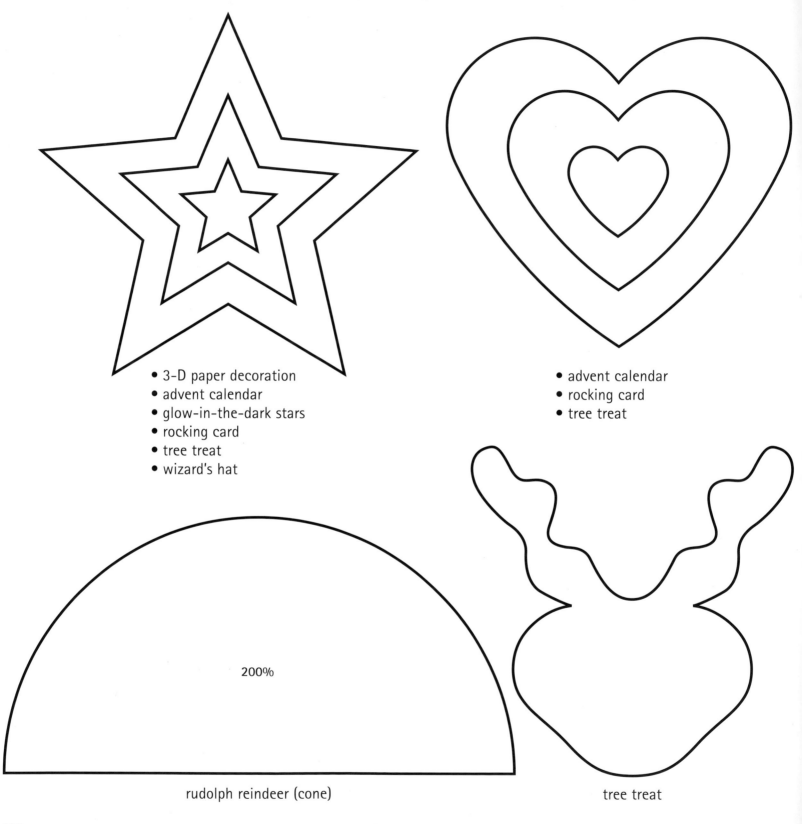

- 3-D paper decoration
- advent calendar
- glow-in-the-dark stars
- rocking card
- tree treat
- wizard's hat

- advent calendar
- rocking card
- tree treat

200%

rudolph reindeer (cone)

tree treat

238

200%

Christmas stocking

3-D paper decoration

- 3-D paper decoration
- advent calendar
- rocking card
- tree treat

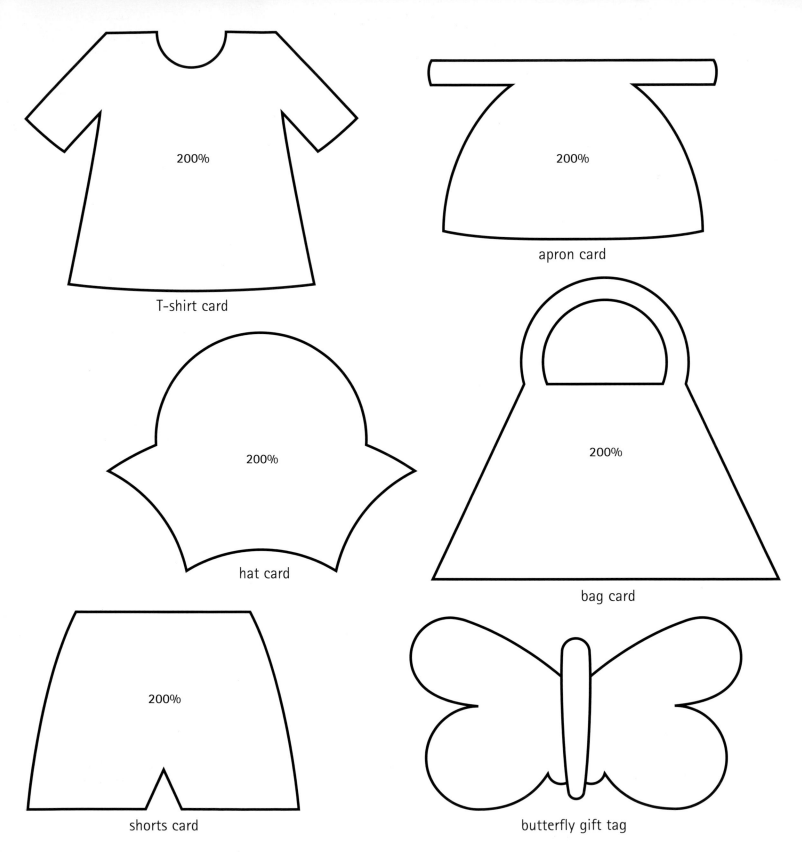

200%

T-shirt card

200%

apron card

200%

hat card

200%

bag card

200%

shorts card

butterfly gift tag

240

- loved-up T-shirt
- sweetheart photo frame
- valentine card

200%

flower photo frame

- colourful flowers
- foam necklace

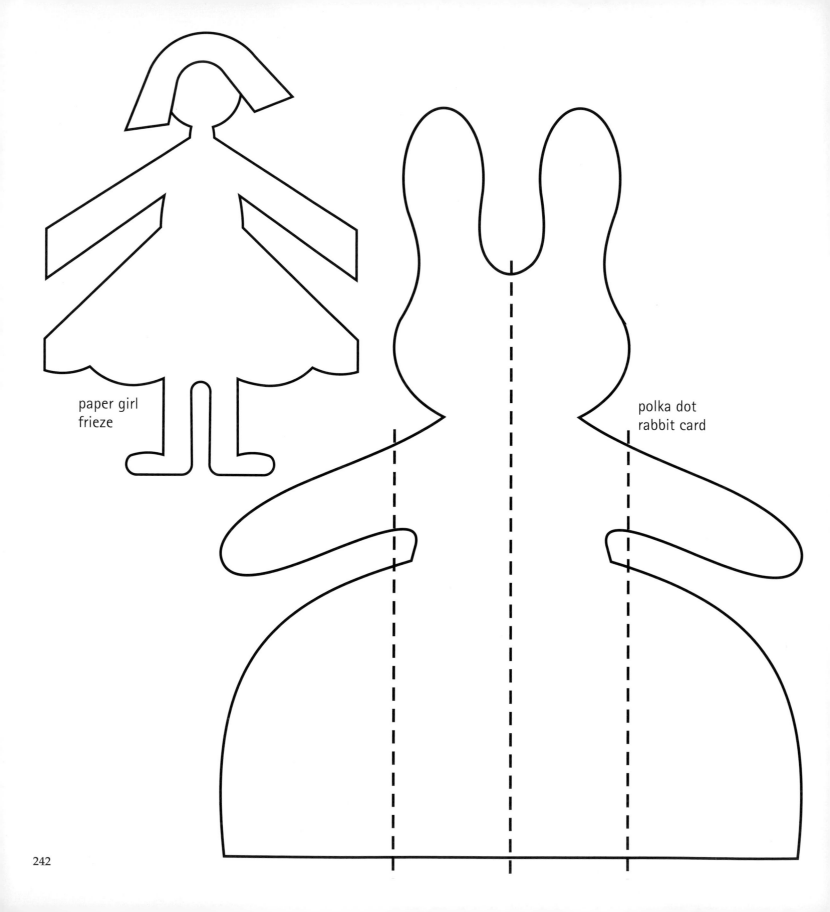

paper girl
frieze

polka dot
rabbit card

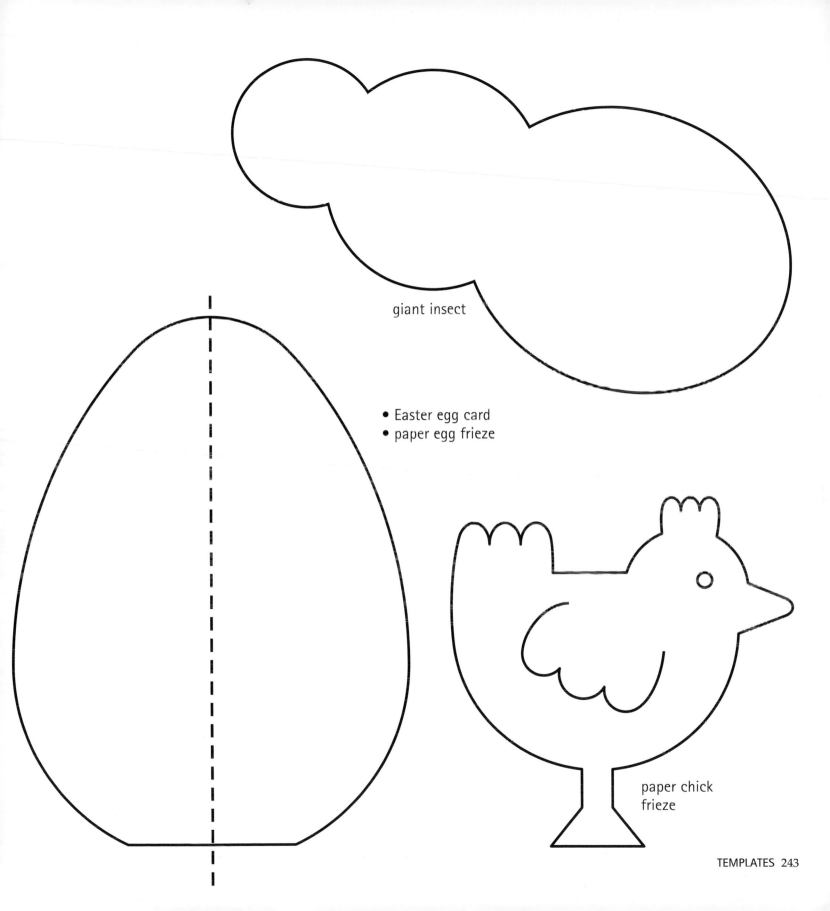

giant insect

• Easter egg card
• paper egg frieze

paper chick
frieze

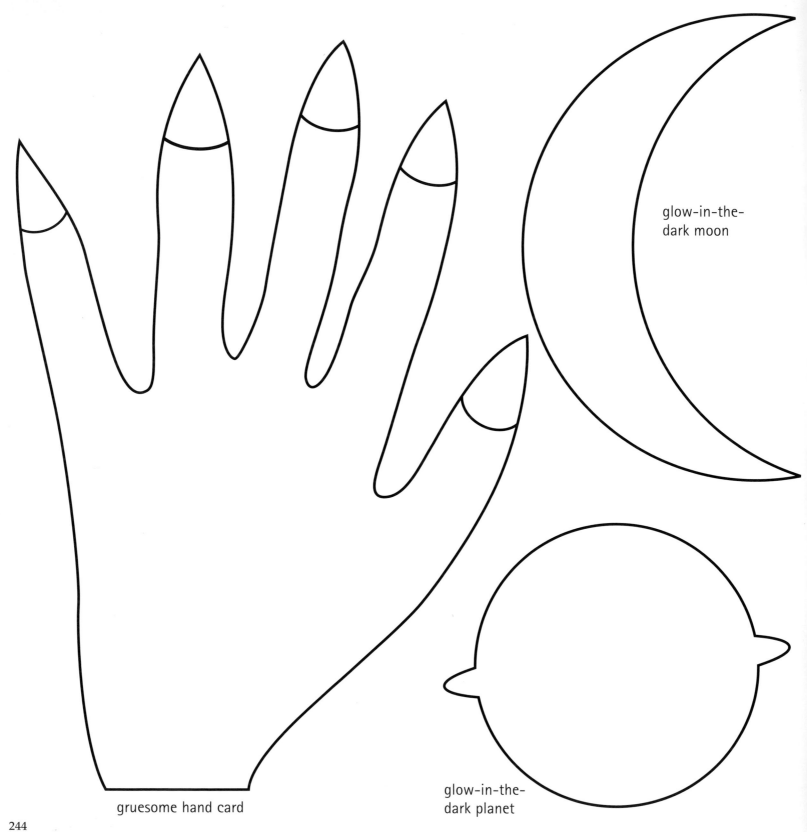

glow-in-the-dark moon

gruesome hand card

glow-in-the-dark planet

244

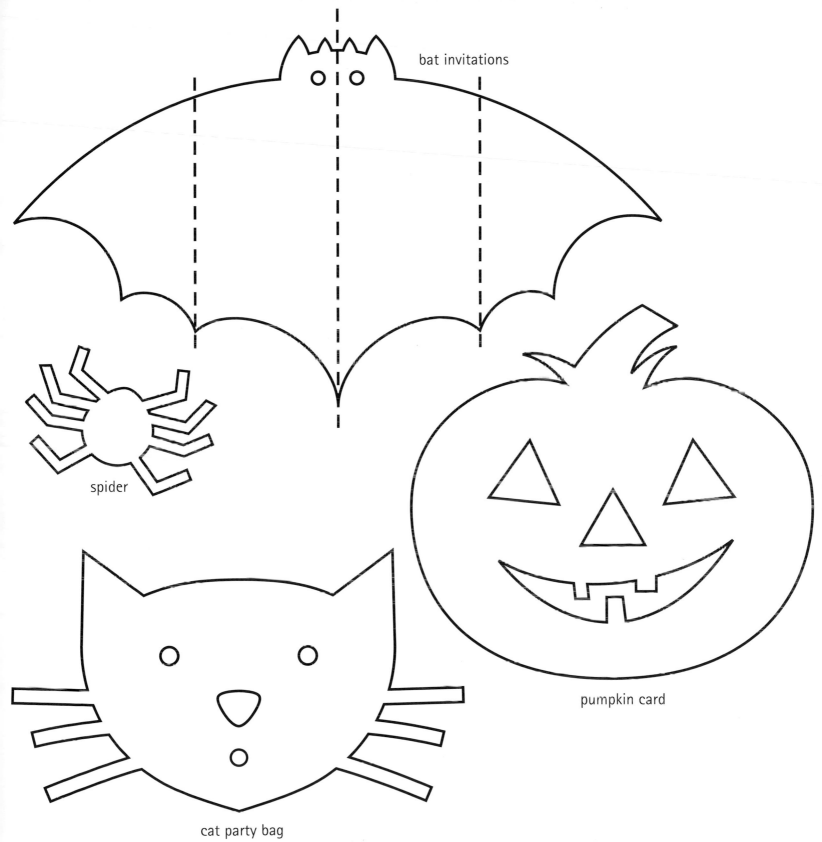

bat invitations

spider

pumpkin card

cat party bag

lavender sprigs

rose bud

bird clock

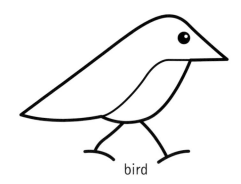

bird

flower

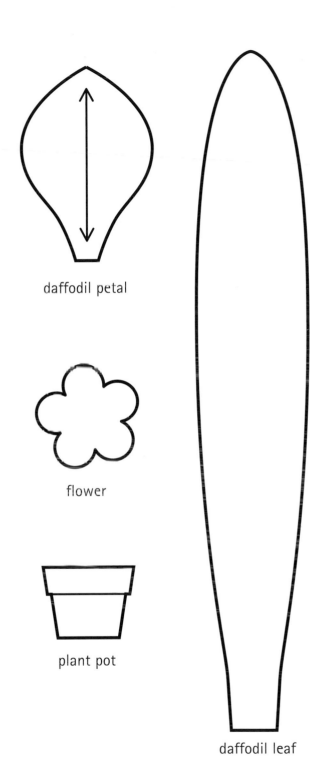

daffodil petal

flower

plant pot

daffodil leaf

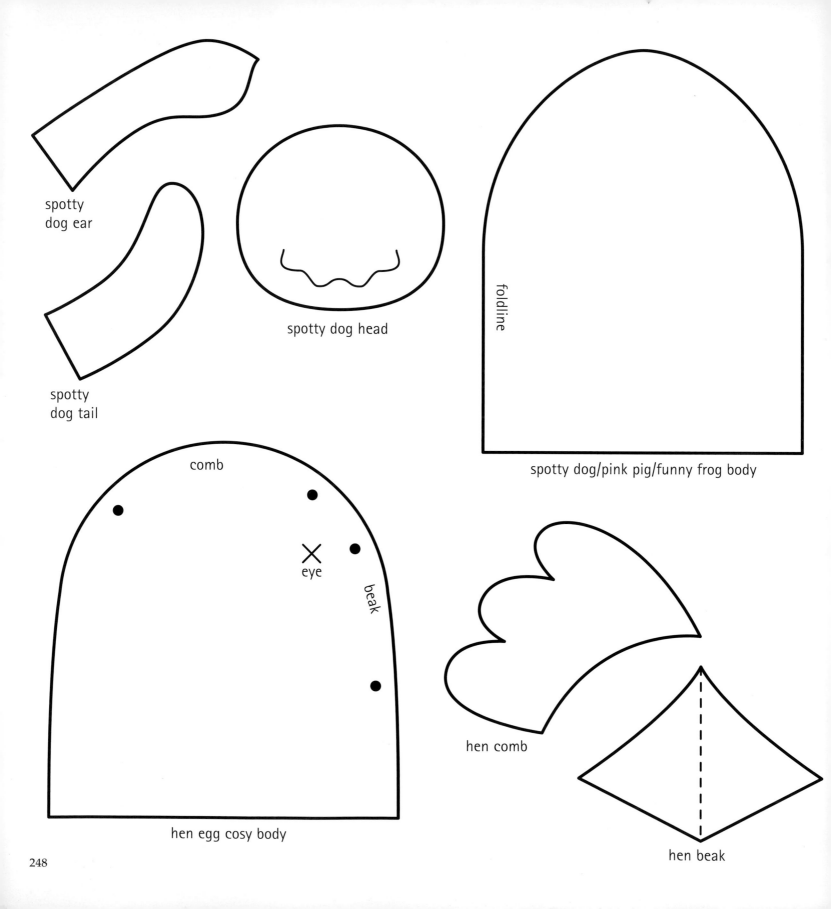

spotty
dog ear

spotty
dog tail

spotty dog head

foldline

spotty dog/pink pig/funny frog body

comb

eye

beak

hen egg cosy body

hen comb

hen beak

248

pig ear

pig head/muzzle

frog head

frog foot

insect wing

oak leaf

cat ear/bird beak

elephant ear

eye patch

tricorn hat

butterfly

lavender
heart
sachet

lavender
sachet
variations

wide cutting line

narrow cutting line

beeswax candle

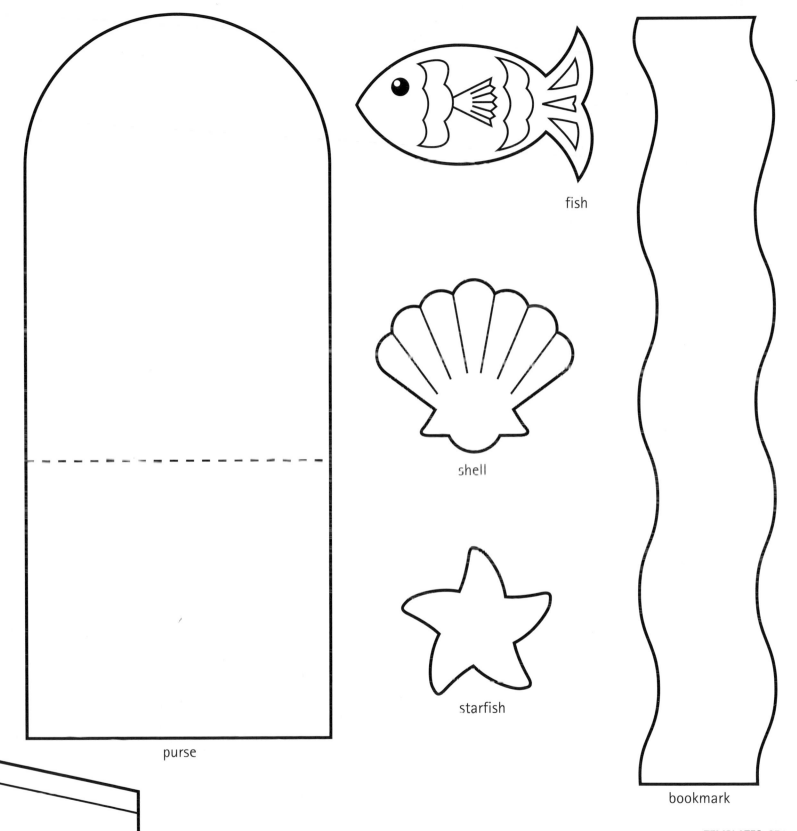

fish

shell

starfish

purse

bookmark

index

acknowledgements

author acknowledgements
Gill Dickinson 14–15, 16–17, 18–19, 20–21, 22–23, 24–25, 26–27, 28–29, 36–37, 42–43, 46–47, 48–49, 52–53, 54–55, 60–61, 62–63, 64–65, 66–67, 68–69, 70–71, 72–73, 74–75, 76–77, 80–81, 82–83, 84–85, 86–87, 88–89, 90–91, 92–93, 96–97, 98–99, 100–101, 102–103, 104–105, 106–107, 108–109, 110–111, 112–113 114–115, 116–117, 118–119, 120–121, 130–131, 132–133, 134–135, 146–147, 164–165, 196–197, 218–219, 220–221, 232–233, 234–235, 238–239, 240–241, 242–243, 244–245.

Sara Lewis 10–11, 202–203, 204–205, 206–207, 208–209, 210–211, 212–213, 226–227, 228–229, 230–231.

Cheryl Owen 6–7, 8–9, 30–31, 32–33, 34–35, 38–39, 40–41, 50–51, 56–57, 58–59, 78–79, 124–125, 126–127, 128–129, 136–137, 138–139, 140–141, 142–143, 148–149, 150–151, 152–153, 154–155, 156–157, 158–159, 160–161, 162–163, 166–167, 168–169, 170–171, 172–173, 174–175, 176–177, 178–179, 182–183, 184–185, 186–187, 188–189, 190–191, 192–193, 194–195, 198–199, 214–215, 216–217, 222–223, 224–225, 246–247, 248–249, 250–251.

picture acknowledgements
Photography © **Octopus Publishing Group Limite**d/Vanessa Davies, Mike Prior, Peter Pugh-Cook.

Executive Editor **Jane McIntosh**
Managing Editor **Clare Churly**
Executive Art Editor **Penny Stock**
Picture Library Manager **Jennifer Veall**
Designer **Ginny Zeal**
Senior Production Controller **Manjit Sihra**